"A thought-provoking book. If you're interested in investment, you should read it – whether you bracket chartism with astrology or not."

Sir Christopher Hogg, Chairman, Reuters

"In Alistair Blair's book, I finally discovered what the chartists were talking about. An excellent guide for non-chartists and, I am sure, for chartists too."

Richard Hughes, Manager of the M&G Recovery Fund

"A compelling and compulsory read for anyone who has experienced the greed and fear of share ownership."

Charles Skinner, Editor, *Management Today*

GUIDE TO
CHARTING

An Analysis for the
Intelligent Investor

Alistair Blair

London · Hong Kong · Johannesburg · Melbourne · Singapore · Washington DC

PITMAN PUBLISHING
128 Long Acre, London WC2E 9AN
Tel: +44 (0)171 447 2000
Fax: +44 (0)171 240 5771

A Division of Pearson Professional Limited

First published in Great Britain in 1996

ISBN 0 273 62520 9

British Library Cataloguing in Publication Data
A CIP catalogue record for this book can be obtained from the British Library.

10 9 8 7 6 5 4 3

Typeset by Pantek Arts, Maidstone, Kent
Printed and bound in Great Britain

The Publishers' policy is to use paper manufactured from sustainable forests.

ABOUT THE AUTHOR

Alistair Blair is an investment journalist. He read PPE at Oxford and completed an MBA at Manchester Business School. He has ten years of practical City experience, having worked at Hill Samuel and Fidelity Investments. A regular contributor to The Investors Chronicle and other national publications, he also runs a small investment fund.

CONTENTS

FOREWORD

Today, more than ever, we need to make our savings and investments work hard for us. Changes to the welfare state – and the likelihood of further changes to come – mean that managing our capital properly is a key factor in financing the purchase of our home, our healthcare, our children's education and – perhaps most important – our retirement planning.

De-regulation of the financial services industry, which began in the 1980s, has led to a sometimes bewildering proliferation of financial products. The quantity and complexity of products mean investors need guidance. True, there is a world of information out there – some of it free, a lot of it cheap – but is it any good?

The *Investors Chronicle* series of investment books – like the weekly magazine – has been produced to help answer that question, with objective and authoritative advice, written from the investor's point of view.

The aim is to provide readers with a practical, jargon-free guide to all areas of personal finance and investment. Thus, whether you are a sophisticated investor, keen to learn more about the DIY approach to investing, or are new to investment, the books will arm you with the facts and the understanding that you need. As such, they should be the natural complement to the high-quality, independent assessment that the magazine aims to provide every week.

MARK VAN DE WEYER, Publisher, *Investors Chronicle*, FT Magazines

PREFACE

Without question, some people have made astonishing amounts of money from studying share price charts (and virtually nothing else) and foretelling whether the shares would rise or fall.

It is equally certain that further astonishing amounts of money have been lost in the same exercise. Sometimes the same people have clocked up both achievements, or just the second. But a few have restricted themselves to the first. And many more strive to do so.

This book is intended to help non-chartist investors understand what chartists do.

Few claims in the world of investment attract more divided views than whether a 'head and shoulders' formation denotes anything more than nothing. Many investors have heard of this and other oddly named tools of the chartists' trade, without understanding them. Even if you see no financial benefit in gaining this understanding, you may well be interested to discover how the other half lives (and if you take in the currency, commodities and derivatives markets, it is probably more than half).

There may well be more books about charting (or 'technical analysis' as it is also known) than there are books about the more conventional approach – fundamental analysis. This book's modest claim to differentiation is that it is not written by a chartist. It tackles the subject from your side of the fence.

Although I have both feet in the fundamentalist's camp, I do not scorn every chartist utterance. A significant fraction, but not all. I do believe that some chartists – a comparative few, indeed – have been remarkably successful over very long periods of time. In the 12 years to 1991, Mr Gil Blake, a small private

US money manager, averaged a 45 per cent annual return. This was not the outcome of a few lucky years combined with many poor ones: his lowest annual return was 20 per cent. All of Mr Blake's investment decisions are derived from technical analysis. In the 1980s, Mint, another US investment management company (but 50-per-cent-owned by the UK firm ED&F Man) achieved annual returns of between 13 and 60 per cent from its trend-following system, which uses a variety of technical analysis methods. Mint has not maintained this performance in the 1990s, but that does not wholly invalidate its earlier record.

Chapter 1 puts charting in perspective. It compares the approach with fundamental analysis and finds a few points of agreement. It deals, only briefly, with the supposed 'crowd psychology' explanation of why charting might work. This book is not a justification of charting, but an exploration.

Chapters 2, 3 and 4 are an account of the chartist's tool box. Here you will find and should be able to get behind everything from a trend line to Welles Wilder's RSI. Chapter 4 includes the complete methods of working out some of the popular mathematical indicators. This is the 'hardest' section of the book and you may wish to skip it on first reading. Worked examples are given which will enable you to set up technical analysis programmes on a computer spreadsheet or, if you have the time, on paper.

Chapters 5 and 6 deal with two specialised forms of charting: Japanese Candlesticks and point and figure charts.

Chapter 7 deals with the prominent charting theories, including Elliott Wave Theory, the Coppock Indicator and the outlandish notions of WD Gann.

Chapter 8 briefly covers a few people who have made documented fortunes from charting techniques. Not all of them hung on to these fortunes.

Chapter 9 is a key part of the book. In most books on the subject, you will find what you may consider an undue preponderance of charts showing successful charting signals: *this head and shoulders heralded a price decline of 50 per cent...* and so on.

But a large fraction of charting signals fail. Chapter 9 includes 12 years of share price graphs for the UK's top 25 quoted companies. Each is examined to show what signals it gave and whether they were successful. You will gain a lot of understanding by working through this chapter.

Chapter 10 gathers together a few conclusions for all investors and considers how you might put charting techniques to use.

'*Mr Market is there to serve you, not to guide you... it will be disastrous if you fall under his influence...*'

Warren Buffet, quoting Benjamin Graham
in *The Berkshire Hathaway Chairman's Letter, 1987*

'*About 20 years ago, I observed that chartists usually had dirty raincoats and large overdrafts. ... Even now, I do not know many rich chartists. However, since those early days, I have met one or two who have made their fortune and read about a few more ...*'

Jim Slater in *The Zulu Principle*

INTRODUCTION

I'm not a chartist. When I make an investment decision, I try to imagine how the facts I'm pondering would look to Warren Buffett. What's the intrinsic value of the company? Does it have exceptional economics? Do these managers think like owners?

And I certainly buy that nugget of wisdom from his teacher, Benjamin Graham, which Buffett quoted in the 1987 Berkshire Hathaway annual report:

> '... imagine market quotations as coming from a remarkably accommodating fellow named Mr Market who is your partner in a private business. Without fail, Mr Market appears daily and names a price at which he will either buy your interest or sell you his.
>
> Even though the business that the two of you own may have economic characteristics that are stable, Mr Market's quotations will be anything but. For, sad to say, the poor fellow has incurable emotional problems. At times he feels euphoric and can see only the favorable factors affecting the business. When in that mood, he names a very high buy–sell price because he fears you will snap up his interest and rob him of imminent gains. At other times he is depressed and can see nothing but trouble ahead for both the business and the world. On these occasions he will name a very low price, since he is terrified that you will unload your interest on him.
>
> Mr Market has another endearing characteristic: he doesn't mind being ignored. If his quotation is uninteresting to you today, he will be back with a new one tomorrow. Transactions are strictly at your option ...
>
> Mr Market is there to serve you, not to guide you. ... it will be disastrous if you fall under his influence ...'
>
> (Reprinted with permission from Warren E. Buffett)

And yet.

The other thought that occurs to me as I check my portfolio is that there often seems to be a pattern in Mr Market's quotations.

At the time of writing, I own shares in Grand Metropolitan, one of the world's biggest branded drinks companies. I bought them because I think earnings will grow and the shares could be in for an upwards rerating. I'm looking for a 50 per cent gain on these shares and I'm not going to sell them until either I've got it, or I conclude that it's not coming, or I find something more attractive into which to switch the money.

In the meantime they're on a little treadmill, as Figure I.1 shows. Up they go to around 455p. Down they go into the 430s. A ceiling and a floor, at least for the present.

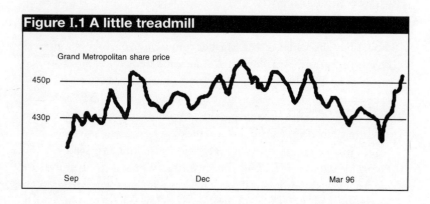

Figure I.1 A little treadmill

Grand Metropolitan share price

These movements do not reflect newsflow: few of them seem to tie up with changes of recommendations by analysts, or positive or negative announcements from the company. I can rationalise that right now the price band – in the lower 400s – is sensible. It puts the company on a rating modestly below the market's. This looks broadly right, given that a seeming majority of commentators do not share my view that its earnings have a good chance of growing strongly over the next year or two.

As a value investor looking for a meaty gain, I'm just not interested in assessing share prices with razor sharp precision. When I say I'm looking for 50 per cent, I mean 40 to 80 per cent. I'm not looking to 'scalp' it. Nor am I going to sell the share if it goes down by 30 per cent, unless some more information turns up to alter my fundamental view.

But someone clearly is trying to scalp it. Someone is buying Grand Met whenever it gets down into the 420s. And someone is selling the share in the 450s.

They could be the same people.

If I practised a different style of investing, I could have made money out of these fluctuations. Not 50 per cent. More like 2 per cent per deal after all expenses including the dealing spread (4p on this share), commission (I have assumed half a per cent) and stamp duty.

Two per cent is 2 per cent, especially if it's earned in a matter of weeks. The average investor is doing well to earn 15 per cent a year on his money, if he does it year in, year out. A few quickly-earned 2 per cents out of Grand Metropolitan would be very useful. And if I had dealt in the right options, instead of the share itself, I might have made more than 2 per cent.

The pattern traced out by Grand Metropolitan's share price is known as 'consolidation', and is just one of scores of patterns that chartists look for. I quote it because it is immediate to me, not because it is an especially good example. In fact the floor and ceiling of this consolidation are probably too close to get most chartists excited. But it serves to make the point that Buffett's approach isn't the only one.

In fact, knowingly or otherwise, most investors attach much more significance to consolidations and other share price patterns than to anything Buffett ever said. To stick with the Buffett style, you have to be very patient. Few of us are.

Nothing demonstrates this more tellingly than the practice of taking profits. Whenever one of my shares has a good day or a good week (say a gain of 5 per cent or more), I'm pretty sure the next thing it will do is move back a little.

You may think this observation borders on the banal but it contains a fundamental truth about investing. *Many investors who have made a little profit would rather realise it than risk losing it.*

Yes, often the price falls back after rising because some investors think the new price overstates future prospects. But this cannot explain every such price move.

Another of my shares is Flying Flowers. This small company uses the postal system to send out sprays of carnations. The sprays are inexpensive at £10 including delivery and are usually sent as gifts. Flying Flowers is a downmarket alternative to Interflora. The company was a new issue in 1993 since when earnings have grown strongly.

The share price has moved up accordingly but the rating is still below the market's. Last week as I write the company reported strong profits growth and a good outlook. I see nothing to suggest that the formula has not got further to go and I doubt whether any shareholders would seriously dissent from this view.

The price moved up around 17 per cent to 159p on the announcement, then slipped a penny. There was plenty of business in the shares, which meant lots of shareholders had decided to cash in their profits. Yet, with earnings of 10.6p just announced, at 159p Flying Flowers was on an historic price earnings ratio of 15, compared with 16.6 for the FT All Share Index.

I would consider selling my Flying Flowers shares if the rating got a long way ahead of earnings prospects – if, say, the price had moved to 250p after the announcement. But what's the point of selling a growth share on a sub-market rating? *The point is*, selling locks in healthy gains. You will sell Flying Flowers in this situation if you fear you might lose the attractive profits you have accumulated in the stock.

Many shareholders are less interested in maximising their gains – should that mean risking a gain already made – than in taking gains when they are available.

This factor is as potent a force in setting share prices as any which guides Warren Buffett. The philosophy of making investment decisions on the basis of share price patterns recognises forces every bit as real as those which are tracked by fundamental analysts. Fear, unthinking greed (as opposed to thinking greed) and the idea of profiting from what the crowd thinks (whether the crowd is right or wrong) are present in at least as many investment decisions as are considerations of intrinsic value and whether the managers think like owners.

And sometimes, despite my best efforts, I see these in myself. I'm pretty good at holding a share for the bigger gain. But I find it difficult to buy a share – whatever the fundamentals – if it looks irredeemably out of favour – the evidence for which would be a share price that has not moved despite positive developments. In such situations, I will wait for the share to bottom out and take a decisive upturn before buying it. Of course, that often means I miss it altogether. What has looked like a bargain for weeks at 100p, somehow doesn't look so attractive if it moves up to 130p in a matter of days.

So this book is a strange beast. It's not written by a dyed-in-the-wool chartist, but a sceptic of the art. But a fascinated sceptic. It is not an explanation of charting – it is an exploration.

I would like to thank Robert Ansted and Mark Harris of the *Investors Chronicle*, Dr John Andrews, Managing Director of Man-GFA AG, Anthony Bolton of Fidelity Investments, Richard Hills of Argyll Investment Management, Elita Caspari, who lent me her cottage in which to write this book, and my wife, Jane, who was very forbearing.

Alistair Blair

'This book is a guide to the techniques used by those who concentrate on price patterns. Such people are known as "chartists" or "technical analysts".'

THE ART OF THE CHART

- ● Fundamental vs technical analysis
- ● The common-sense appeal
- ● Non-equity investments
- ● Selling short
- ● A psychological explanation?

If you want to invest in shares or any other investment, you need a way of making buying and selling decisions. Astrologers, coin tossers and those claiming divine guidance all get a look-in from time to time, but most professionals use one of – or mix – two approaches. They look at fundamentals or price patterns.

This book is a guide to the techniques used by those who concentrate on price patterns. Such people are known as 'chartists' or 'technical analysts', two terms which will be used interchangeably. Chartists are in a significant minority, at least amongst professionals in the stockmarkets. A big stockbroking firm would typically have dozens of fundamental analysts on its staff for each technical analyst it employed. Indeed many top firms don't employ any technical analysts. It's important at the outset to consider why.

FUNDAMENTAL ANALYSIS

'Fundamental analysis' means sifting through the factors that determine a company's future profits as a starting point in deciding whether its share price is cheap or expensive. The starring role in any fundamental analysis goes to the profit forecast, but this is only the tip of the iceberg. Figure 1.1 outlines some of the questions which most fundamental analysts will at least consider before deciding whether a company's shares are a good buy.

Fundamental analysis has many shortcomings, not least that it piles estimate upon estimate then lathers the whole heap with subjectivity. Who's to say the managers are skilled? They might have done well in last year's conditions, but times are forever a-changing. Few proponents regard fundamental analysis as hard science, but would say that like many other disciplines, it's the best we can do. Fundamental analysis also tallies with common sense. Most people, no matter how inexperienced they were in investment analysis, would reckon that the obvious starting point is to try to work out whether the company they were thinking of investing in will prosper.

Figure 1.1 Fundamental questions: what the (pure) chartist ignores

Is the economy heading up or down?
Is the sector in which the firm operates likely to follow a different path from the economy as a whole?
Does the firm have anything going for it? For instance: • a really impressive product • superior marketing • skilled management • built-in growth* *'ClevaNuShops', a new kind of shop, has opened in five towns and been very successful. All other things being equal (and they never are) ClevaNuShops will grow simply by 'rolling out' new shops in other towns. For obvious reasons, an investment which should grow in this way is, on the face of it, attractive. ClevaNuShops could be a better investment than another retailer which runs its nationwide chain of shops exceedingly well but is past its roll-out phase.
Based on all the above and on past experience, what profits will the firm make this year and next?
Do I have enough information to estimate the picture further out too?
Based on my profit forecast, what will earnings per share be? To get earnings per share or 'EPS', subtract tax and sometimes other items from pre-tax profits. Divide the result by the number of shares which the company has in issue.
Based on EPS, what is the price/earnings ratio? The share price divided by EPS. The price/earnings ratio is also known as 'PER', 'PE', 'p/e' or 'rating'. *Price/earnings ratios are very important because they allow direct comparisons of individual shares. For instance GEC has a current year PE ratio (as I write) of 16 whereas Asda's is 13.* In other words, if both companies continue to earn the same profits in future (and don't issue any more shares), it would take 16 years for GEC to earn the amount of money you would pay for one of its shares, but only 13 years for Asda to do the same. Asda appears to be cheaper. As you can see, PE ratios are outrageously simplistic. However, no-one has yet devised an equally

straightforward, but better, method of comparing share prices. *But they are confusing. You need to know which year's profits the PE ratio is based on. It's a common mistake to compare one firm's historic PE with another's forecast PE.*

Can I work out price earnings ratios for future years?
Only if future profits have been estimated.

On the basis of the company's expected future growth of earnings and dividends, and its PE ratio compared with those of similar firms, are its shares cheap or expensive?
You'd pay more (in the form of a higher PE ratio) for a firm which was expected to grow its profits faster, especially if you thought this would continue to be the case.

Is the firm financially sound?
A company can be highly profitable but financially stretched (or unprofitable but stuffed with assets that it could sell for more than its shares are worth). The fundamental analyst will look at a company's balance sheets to check that it is not borrowing too much (this is known as being 'overgeared') and that it generally has the resources to sustain its profitability and to cope with setbacks.

TECHNICAL ANALYSIS

But there is another way. Try technical analysis. To the committed technical analyst, estimates of future profits are a waste of time. In fact in theory and in practice, the process can be carried out even without knowing the identity of the investment. Consider Figure 1.2. It's full of technical significance. To most chartists, it screams 'buy'. Even you, the beginner may be able to appreciate this. If you do, note that you don't know the profits outlook, management competence or even the firm's identity.

Now in fact it's rare for a technical analyst totally to eschew all reference to the fundamentals. But it's worthwhile recognising at the outset that some do.

And this emphasis on price history as opposed to the fundamentals may help you recognise why charting is seen by some fundamental analysts as akin to tea-leaf reading. Further,

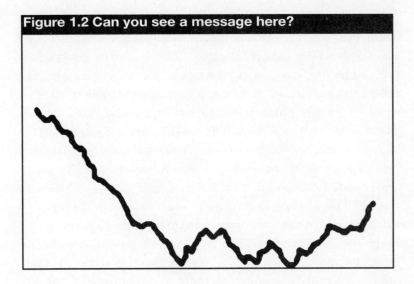

Figure 1.2 Can you see a message here?

technical analysts are wont to point to totally unexpected events in the life of a company with the observation, 'Well, it had to happen, because the chart said it would.' Just before I started to write this book, I interviewed Robin Griffiths, one of London's best-known technical analysts. The week before, Inchcape, the international trading company and UK importer of Toyota cars, had taken the market aback with a profits warning. Its shares were hammered. Griffiths had not forecast Inchcape's difficulties but having looked at its chart after the event, felt that a problem of some sort had been inevitable because its chart was due for a downleg. This 'even the unexpected is predetermined' view of the world is anathema to fundamental analysts.

'How can you begin to consider an investment without putting primary emphasis on its future profitability?' say the sceptics. 'We can, because our systems work,' say the chartists. This assertion raises the hairs on the back of a fundamentalist's neck. 'And furthermore,' goes on the chartist, 'when did you last beat the index?' The observation stings many fundamentalists into silence.

NOT SO DIVIDED AFTER ALL?

Most of the time, though, the two schools co-exist in a spirit of live and let live, sometimes verging on active co-operation. The oft-heard recommendation from a fundamental analyst, 'Buy on weakness,' sounds akin to the sort of injunction that a chartist would issue. Another weakness on the fundamental side is their frequent readiness to issue buy or sell recommendations based on slim value discrepancies. For instance: 'Buy X because it is 20 per cent undervalued compared with Y and Z and this gap should be closed.' This kind of recommendation stems from the fact that stockbrokers' livelihoods depend on investors buying and selling shares, not on buying and *holding* them. They need to find arguments to persuade investors to shuffle their portfolios. If there are no compelling arguments, then an uncompelling one will have to do.

Many people with experience of stockmarket investing and who take their decisions on the basis of the fundamentals would consider the prospect of a 20 per cent gain as simply not tempting. However, from the point of view of a technical analyst, this sort of prospect sounds quite attractive. He uses short horizons and can be happy to win lots of modest share price gains: 'Let's collect this scalp and then move on to the next one.'

Moreover, even the most hardened fundamental analysts acknowledge the importance of 'timing'. Timing is the matter of whether the market as a whole is soundly valued or not. It's relatively easy to compare two shares and come to a conclusion about whether one looks significantly cheaper than the other. But what if, whilst there is a worthwhile disparity in the two shares' values, both, and all the other shares which form the background against which the decision is being made, are over- or under-valued? Here, you have the issue of market timing.

Fundamental analysts tend to address market timing by asking themselves whether the market's rating (i.e., the average

PE ratio across all shares) is out of line with historic norms. This can sound suspiciously close to the chartists' argument that what has gone before is a pointer to what's going to happen next.

And there is a tool called 'beta' which most fundamental analysts are happy to use even though it comes straight out of a share's price graph. Beta is a measure of volatility, that is, of how much a share will move for a given move in the market. Betas tend to fall in the range 0.5 to 2 (although some shares have much higher ones, and they can occasionally be negative). A share with a beta of 0.5 will tend to move half as much as the market. Thus if the market moves up by 10 per cent, Yak PLC with a beta of 0.5, will move up 5 per cent. But consider Zebra PLC, whose beta is 2. Should the market move by 5 per cent, Zebra's price will supposedly change by 10 per cent. That's the theory at any rate. Many high-grade pieces of fundamental research include a share's beta as simply another routine statistic, alongside dividend yield and the price earnings ratio, noting that each industry tends to have a fairly standard beta, and it's best to know what this is before you invest in it.

But where does beta come from? From a painstaking day by day study of how a share price moved compared with how the market moved on that day. Average out your calculations for three or five years and you have your beta.

How do you use beta? Typically you will take a whole portfolio and calculate its average beta. This gives a measure of how volatile your portfolio is, and how well-positioned it is against your expectations for the market. Expecting the market to decline, you might judge your portfolio beta to be rather high and weed out a few of the highest beta shares. If you anticipated an advance in the market, you might instead weed out the lower beta shares. None of this has much to do with the fundamental value of a share. So what is it doing in the fundamentalist's tool kit? True, many of them would regard it as a pretty minor piece of equipment, but it's there all the same. Beta is a grey area where fundamental analysts somewhat sheepishly find themselves meeting up with the technical fraternity.

Perhaps the most compelling argument for the chartists is the one that would appeal to any student of the roulette wheel. If you had seen eight blacks come up in a row, would you bet on red? No? How about 16 blacks or 32? The statistician, here in the guise of the fundamentalist of the roulette table, can give you good evidence that even if there have been 32 blacks in a row, the odds stay even for the next turn of the wheel. Unlike you, the wheel has no memory – it could as easily be black as red. But just as most people would consider that analysis of a company's value should start with its future profitability, so those same people would at some point yield to the argument that red's a good bet – even those who appreciate the statistician's argument.

Many of the recommendations which emanate from technical analysis are parallel to this common sense view that after 32 blacks, red is a good bet. In the past, observes the technical analyst, seven times out of ten when we have had event X (a run of 32 blacks or a 'triple bottom'), then it has been followed by event Y (a red, or a share price rise). Now, we've just had event X, so let's bet on Y.

'Seven times out of ten,' you'll note. The chartist is quite prepared to be wrong, moreso than the fundamentalist. This is normally recognised by the advice, fairly standard alongside technical recommendations, that the trader (probably a more appropriate term than 'investor' for those driven by charts), at the same time as buying into Yak PLC, simultaneously puts in place arrangements to sell if what actually happens to its share price is the opposite of what was expected. This is known as the 'stop-loss' order and takes the form: 'Buy Yak at 200p, anticipating a share price rise. However, instruct your broker to sell them should the price go down below 170p, because if it does, the expected rise above 200p is unlikely to happen.'

The idea of a 'stop-loss' has great appeal to many commonsensical investors. Not everyone has the wisdom or patience of Warren Buffett, and the accompanying confidence that if a share's price goes down after they have bought it, then more of the shares should be bought. Many people want the fun and satisfaction of investing their money directly instead of handing it over to a unit trust manager. They do not have the time or the ability to appraise an investment so that its prospects are beyond doubt at the time they put their money into it. Moreover, they know they have these shortcomings. Maybe they 'should' put more time and effort into analysis, but the fact is, they don't. Against this background, the idea of selling a losing investment has lots of appeal.

Selling an investment for no other reason than that in the short term its price has fallen should be anathema to any fundamental investor. It's pure chartism (or sometimes, it's lazy or nervous fundamentalism). But many people do just this. This is a group of people who might as well get wise to technical analysis, even if they think of it as tea leaves.

Despite its apparently scientific attention to unarguable facts – past prices – as opposed to the often subjective analysis carried out by fundamentalists, technical analysis is more like art than science. Just as Picasso and Rembrandt would have delivered up strikingly different images of the same figure, so you can find technical analysts who will give you wholly different interpretations of the same price histories. They all talk in terms of 'triple bottoms', 'upswings', 'consolidations' and 'breakouts', just as Picasso and Rembrandt would have agreed on reds, blues and yellows. But what's a triple bottom? What portends a breakout? Make no mistake, here just as in every other professional endeavour, you'll find as much disagreement as agreement. Technical analysts use a huge number of indicators to arrive at their conclusions. Look through the central chapters of this book, and you will find: oscillators, trend lines, relative strength indicators, point and figure charts, candlesticks, and many more (and this book just scratches the surface). Each has adherents. Others use a combination. It should not be surprising that chartists offer up different conclusions.

SURELY, IF THESE PATTERNS ARE SO OBVIOUS, YOU CAN'T PROFIT FROM THEM?

Can technical analysis be self-defeating? It's often said that a system designed to beat the market cannot work once the market as a whole starts to use it. But an excellent example of this argument at work comes right from the fundamentalists' camp. During the 1980s, the attractions of small companies were regularly espoused by commentators who pointed out that a portfolio kept in a random selection of small shares since the 1950s would have far outperformed one composed of market leaders. Small companies should be more capable of serious growth than larger companies, went one of the explanations for this effect. Apparently, this characteristic outweighed the fact that small companies are weaker than large ones and therefore also more likely to falter. There were many launches of unit and investment trusts designed to capitalise on 'the small companies effect'.

But in the 1990s the small companies sector disappointed. These new trusts sank to the bottom of the performance tables. One explanation was that small companies were less suited to those recessionary times than their larger brethren. But another was that the historical pattern was bound to disappear as soon as it was discovered. All that money which was diverted into small companies' shares could not fail to lift their share prices relative to other sectors. This very act corrected the anomaly. After that it was impossible to profit from it.

It will be years before this argument can be concluded. However, the second explanation deserves attention. It is easy to see that once an anomaly has been ironed out, it is of no use to investors.

So, doesn't the same go for chart patterns? In many cases, precisely the opposite, in fact. The problem may be not that the market latches on to them, but that it fails to do so. Many a chart signal fails because what's supposed to happen does so, but tardily. Charting is an attempt to profit by forecasting a relatively short-term price movement. The chartist stands before the supposed movement, and says, 'This is what's going to happen next.' If the market climbs on to his bandwagon, his forecast becomes self-fulfilling. His shorter investment horizons would save him from putting long-term money into a once-in-a-lifetime discovery such as the small company effect. Unless he could get in before the market latched on to it. By contrast, the huge quantity of money that went into attempts to capitalise on the small companies effect was 'after the event'.

Nonetheless, it is true that a good signal, which has worked often, will start to fail if everyone begins to use it. The chartist recognises this. He uses lots of signals, putting aside any that seem to have stopped working, and reintroducing previously 'worn out' ones if they seem to show renewed promise.

THE STOCKMARKET IS NOT WHERE YOU'LL FIND MOST CHARTISTS

This book deals with charting in relation to investing in shares. However, the great bulk of chartists are to be found not in the stockmarket but in the currency and commodities markets. The international currency markets are much larger than any stockmarket, and are far more liquid (that is, they see much more turnover, or trading). Trading of the D-mark against the dollar or of either against the pound or yen exceeds the turnover in any share, with trading in just 12 currency cross-markets (yen/dollar, pound/D-mark, etc) worldwide estimated at over $700 bn a day. This figure does not include trading of currency derivatives such as futures and options. By contrast, the New York Stock Exchange sees turnover of $40 bn on a busy day, and that is spread across 3,000 or more stocks. Turnover on the London Stock Exchange is worth around £3–4 bn daily ($6 bn).

OPTIONS, FUTURES AND INDEXES

If you are going to receive a worthwhile amount of some foreign currency in the future – say dollars from your US customer – you may want to avoid ('hedge against' or just 'hedge') the possibility that when the dollars arrive, the exchange rate has moved against you (i.e., that your dollars convert into fewer pounds than you had been anticipating). You can avoid this risk in several ways, but the commonest these days is to use one of the international financial futures exchanges, such as LIFFE. Here, paying very low commissions, you can can get a price today for dollars you won't receive until some date in the future. The low cost of dealing and the immense liquidity of these markets even for huge transactions mean that they are used not only by people with 'genuine' needs to exchange currencies, such as companies receiving payments for exports, but also by money managers who are responsible for looking after large pools of money. These include government agencies, such as the Saudi Arabian Monetary Authority and private funds (such as George Soros' Quantum Fund) whose *raison d'être* is to make money by speculating on movements in currencies and anything else they think might offer the opportunity of a profit. Other players include banks, which, as well as operating in these markets on behalf of customers, also dedicate some of their own money to speculating in these financial futures. Proprietary trading, it's called. Anyone from Barings could tell you all about it.

Interest rate movements too are covered by these financial futures markets. Suppose that instead of a foreign currency, you are going to receive a large payment in your own currency. In, say, a year's time. You won't be spending it immediately and will want to earn interest on it for a few months. Of course, interest rates move up and down just like currencies. You don't want to be a prisoner of next year's interest rate: you'd like to know, today, what interest rate you're going to get next year. No problem. The same financial futures exchanges also offer contracts which will enable you to secure a rate today for next year's (or next month's) money. All the same players: banks, international companies, government agencies and private funds operate in interest rate markets too.

There is also outstanding liquidity in the trading of commodities such as soya beans, orange juice, oil, gas and metals and in stock index futures – these allow you to protect yourself against, or bet on, future movements in Stock Exchange Indices such as the FT-SE 100 and the S&P 500. To the average UK private stockmarket investor, these may seem weird investment areas. But the turnover in many of them, on exchanges such as the Chicago Mercantile Exchange and the Chicago Board of Trade and the London Metal Exchange, more than rivals that for most shares.

In addition to futures contracts, the same exchanges and players also offer 'options' contracts which work in a slightly different way. For most investors, the essence of an option is that the buyer has to complete only if it is in his favour to do so. The opposite applies to option sellers (also known as 'option writers'). They are only ever called upon to complete the deal when it is not in their favour to do so; in return, they get the price of the option whether the buyer completes or not.

Take the dollar payment you are going to receive from your US customer. It's due in 90 days. You can buy a futures contract today which enables you to fix the value of your future payment at $1.38. Buy it, and you will lock into this rate. But you may think the dollar will be stronger than that. In that case, you could buy an option. This is available at $1.40. It's more expensive than the futures contract because it offers you extra flexibility which doesn't come free. Now, if your own feelings turn out to be right and the dollar does indeed strengthen, to say $1.32, you can forget about the option contract and sell your dollars at $1.32. But if you were wrong and the dollar instead weakened to say $1.44, you're protected by your option. Using this, you sell at $1.40 and convert into a higher amount of pounds than you would have got at $1.44 (which will be lessened, however, by the amount you paid to buy the option).

Trading in options is meat and drink to any regular participant in the currency, commodity and index markets.

Exchange rates can be confusing to anyone who doesn't deal in them regularly. A good rhyme to have in mind is 'Hello, Bye-bye – Sell low, Buy high'. Figure 1.3 gives a summary of the above.

Figure 1.3 Sell low, buy high

Assume the dollar payment was $10 m:

If you sold these dollars at	$1.44, you receive	£6.944 m
or at	$1.40 ...	£7.143 m (less cost of option)
...	$1.38 ...	£7.246 m
...	$1.32 ...	£7.576 m (less cost of option)

WHERE FUNDAMENTALISTS WRING THEIR HANDS

Apart from being bigger, these three arenas – currencies, interest rates and commodities, traded in either 'spot', futures or options forms – also share another characteristic which distinguishes them from stockmarkets. This is that the translation of fundamental factors into prices tends to be a much fuzzier process than is true in the stockmarket (and it is pretty fuzzy there). For instance, a currency's value against other currencies should, on the face of it, depend upon whether the country's imports exceed its exports, how much money its government is borrowing, and the rate of interest available to people who hold money in that currency. These factors and the expectations about how they will change in the future 'should' be the crucial determinants of a currency's value, just as earnings per share and other fundamentals go to explain the price of a company's shares.

Now, it is certainly true that earnings per share, especially in the short term, can be but poorly related to that share's price. Nonetheless, over a two- or three-year time frame, marked changes in the former tend to lead to marked changes in the latter. In currencies, however, the time frame required for marked changes in fundamentals to translate into prices is often much longer. None of the three supposed drivers – the balance of imports against exports, government borrowing and interest rates – exerts the same pull on currencies as earnings per share does upon a share price. Currencies with atrocious trade and debt deficits have been known to overcome all selling pressures for years by keeping interest rates at attractive levels. In theory, the downwards pressure from the first two problems 'should not' have been counterbalanced by the generous interest rate on offer. But they often have been. At other times, a huge hike in interest rates (such as the one implemented by the British government the day it was ejected from the European Monetary System) fails to convince: the currency falls nonetheless.

Perhaps it is because of this difficulty of interpreting how the fundamentals in these markets will affect currency, interest rate and commodity values, that it is in these areas, not in the stockmarkets, where you will find the vast majority of chartists. Another explanation put forward is that because of their immense liquidity, these markets display the characteristic patterns looked for by chartists more frequently than the less liquid stockmarkets. If you're looking for a certain price wiggle that signals a profit opportunity, it's best to look in a place where prices wiggle often. Many professional traders in these markets carry out 'intra-day' trading – that is, they work from charts which show minute-by-minute changes in prices, and aim to be in and out of an investment within hours or less. In comparison, share prices are sloth-like. Share price patterns emerge in days or weeks, not hours.

With these enormous markets comprised in large measure of chartists, all looking for chart patterns and knowing that their fellow chartists are doing the same, and moreover making a living out of it, it is difficult to support the assertion that chart patterns are useless as soon as the market latches on to them. The market knows all about them already.

However, as mentioned above, different chartists use different indicators, or different combinations of indicators. A professional chartist would not see a triple bottom as an investment opportunity. He might want to see it accompanied by, say, a rise in turnover (which he calls 'volume'), improving momentum and followed by a golden cross. Now, here you have a trading system that can be devalued by widespread adoption. If the combination of these four indicators has turned into a profit opportunity several times in the recent past on the pork bellies (also known as 'bacon') market of the Chicago Mercantile Exchange, every chartist there will know all about it. The result will be that the next time the first three occur, many won't wait for the golden cross. They will anticipate it by buying pork bellies now. What was a four-indicator signal becomes a three-indicator signal. But whoever settled upon the four indicator version, if he has been sticking to his tried and tested system, will be disappointed. As he waits for the fourth crucial indicator – the one that sealed the decision to buy – he finds it has already happened in the twinkling of an eye after the third.

Chartists who use complex indicators like this one have to anticipate that the market will steal their findings if they are at all successful. And adapt.

But simpler indicators endure. The triple bottom, pure and simple, is not in the same league as a complex indicator. If you looked hard, you would find dozens of examples in a few years of share price histories. It's too fleeting, too regular and too often unsuccessful to attract a great pile of money into its next occurrence. But those with the patience to look out for 'good ones' can, they believe, nevertheless turn them to their advantage.

CHARTISTS DO IT UP *AND* DOWN

A central part of the chartist philosophy is the belief that falling share prices can be as profitable as rising ones, and this is another point of differentiation from the fundamentalist approach. It's not that the latter doesn't expect share prices ever to fall. Rather, their longer investment horizons make it more difficult for them to turn expectation into profit. Fundamental analysis of a company may conclude that its shares are overvalued, but will not normally uncover a timetable according to which the share price will fall.

There are two ways of profiting from the belief that a share price will fall: selling shares you do not have (known as 'selling short'), or buying a put option. Selling shares you do not have is a very short-term tool and is only genuinely available to large investors. A 'sell' deal can be settled by borrowing shares, but this involves hefty costs. You would have to be anticipating a considerable, and preferably quick, fall in the share price to enter into a share borrowing transaction.

A put option allows you to sell shares at a future date (the 'strike date') at a price fixed today (the 'strike price'). Like the options available on the financial futures exchanges, a stock option is a deal you can walk away from if that suits you. The London Traded Options Market (part of LIFFE) offers options on a variety of strike prices and strike dates for the 100 or so leading shares on the Stock Exchange. If Blue Chip PLC is currently trading at 300p, you could buy an option to sell it at 275p, 250p or 225p with strike dates in three, six or nine months' time. You can also buy options on all other shares, using the traditional options market operated by the Stock Exchange. This is less flexible, offering only a single strike price (today's share price) and a single strike date (in three months' time). Nonetheless, it allows you to back your judgement that a share price is due for a fall (or a rise: 'call' options are the opposite of puts: they work in exactly the same way and are used by people expecting a share price to rise).

If you think the price will fall further than the difference between today's price and the strike price (and by more than the cost of the option), then you can buy the put option and wait for the share price to fall. Assuming it does, you would then buy the shares in the normal way at the lower price and immediately sell them at the higher strike price to whoever had sold you the option ('the option writer'). In fact, in the traded options market, you don't go through the rigmarole of buying the shares and selling them to your option writer. Instead, the market simply pays you the profit you would have made had you done so. See Figure 1.4 for an example of how this works.

Figure 1.4 How a put option works

Blue Chip PLC

Today's share price	500p
Three-month put option over 1,000 shares:	
Strike price	475p per share
Option price	£100
Three months later, the share price turns out to be	420p

Your profit:
The difference between the strike price and the actual price on the strike date,

i.e., 475p – 420p	=	55p
Multiplied by 1,000 shares	=	£550
Less cost of option	=	£100
Profit		£450

This is all very well except, from the fundamentalist's point of view, in the little matter of timescales. Assuming you are not using borrowed money which has to be repaid by a set date, buying a share and holding it allows you to profit (if the share rises) without worrying at all about timescales. The fundamentalist isn't banking that the shares he buys this month will rise next month, over the next three months, or perhaps indeed over the next year. He just expects them to rise. Period. He didn't say when.

Yes, it's wonderful if the rise happens sooner rather than later, but he recognises that it could take time. Of course, he takes the same attitude towards shares that he thinks will go down in value.

Now you can see why profiting from share price falls is a province the chartists pretty much have to themselves. The chartist, you will remember, says, 'This is what's going to happen next.' He's quite happy to back his judgement by buying a put option, because he thinks 'next' means in the next few weeks or months.

Of course, the world is not as black and white as this. Plenty of fundamentalists buy options. Whilst most of the time they don't want to make judgements about timescales, from time to time, they will have a firm conviction that a share is due for a serious short term price adjustment. And when they do, they will seek to profit from this judgement by buying an option.

BUYERS, SELLERS, FEAR, GREED, AND PSYCHOLOGY

Why does or should technical analysis work?

Explanations usually centre on the 'the psychology of buyers and sellers,' and in particular, the price at which they bought their shares. This is another piece of the chartist compendium that should strike a chord in the mind of the sceptical observer.

What is the significance of the price at which you bought your shares? It determines the profit or loss you will make on your transaction. And that's that. Isn't it? Of what significance today is your buying price of six weeks ago? Nil. What matters today is today's price and the company's and the market's prospects as of today. To the rational and cool-minded investor, the price at which he originally bought his shares should be his-tory. He should get up every morning and review his investments anew. Today, they're a 'buy', 'sell' or 'hold' at today's prices. The buying price is irrelevant. Isn't it?

But if you believe all that then presumably you've never given a moment's thought to stock advice such as, 'Secure some profits now by selling half your holding.' Who is as cool as to ignore his buying price? For every investor who operates on the 'cool and rational' principle, there must be 1,000 who do not. Of course the buying price is important, and even the rational cool-minded investor knows this. You bought shares in Red Chip at 250p. They've been to 140p, but have now recovered to 250p. They're set to continue rising. But what goes up can go down, as it did, so painfully, before. The choice is simple. Get out now and get your money back. Or hold on for the profit you were expecting when you first bought them. The 'profit' that turned out to be a loss last time you were here.

Now, it's certainly not the case that there will be 1,000 sellers for every holder. But there will be 1,000 who go through this thought process, and plenty of them will decide to get out. Here, fear wins. And many of them went through the same thinking three weeks ago when Red Chip was at 220p. They decided to hang on just a little longer to see if they could get all their money back rather than just most of it. Then, greed won.

Even though it 'shouldn't' be, the price at which people buy shares is often significant in a subsequent decision to sell them. Chartists know this very well and seek to profit from it.

Example

Every now and again, share price patterns emerge which reveal that particular prices have special significance for the shares in question. Figure 1.5 shows an example.

A technical analysis of this chart might run as follows:

Investors who held the shares all the way up to 900p in January 1994 are, by March, disappointed that they didn't sell at the peak. It's been a memorable run and that nice round figure sticks in their minds. They resolve to sell if ever they see it or anything else close to it again. These investors will set up 'resistance' at 900p, by

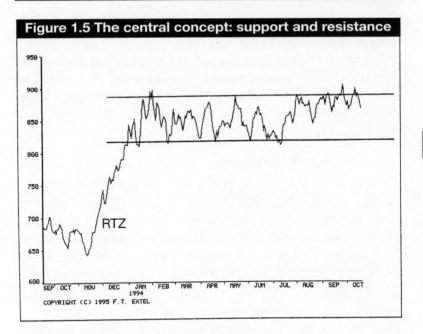

Figure 1.5 The central concept: support and resistance

RTZ

COPYRIGHT (C) 1995 F.T. EXTEL

1

selling their shares at that price and preventing them from advancing past it, until they've sold out.

At the same time, other investors who sold out at 820–850p on that sharp pullback in January are disappointed that they sold too early. These investors decide to buy RTZ back if ever the shares come down to their selling price. In March, they get the opportunity. They have set up 'support'.

Now, there's an oscillation between the two camps. In the low 800s, out come the buyers who were disappointed not to have had the full run. For months, they can be relied upon to come back and support the share price at that level. But as the price approaches 900p, investors who have seen this price before and failed to bank it aren't going to pass up the opportunity too often in the coming months. There they go in April and May, and again in August and September, selling out and so preventing the share price from breaking out above 900p. By this time, they are supplemented by a third group: those who bought in at 900p. These are the investors who correspond to the Red Chip shareholder described above. To them, it now looks less likely that this share price is going anywhere serious, soon. Just as with the first group, 900p has become the price at which they will sell.

The chartist should have been able to identify these support and resistance levels by say May, or June at the latest. Now he has an opportunity to profit. Buy at 820p, sell at 880p. Still better, wait for one or other level to be broken, because when that happens, 'This is what's going to happen next.'

Another explanation for how particular prices can become significant would lie in the buying and selling decisions of institutional shareholders. When a fund manager decides to invest in a company, he will very likely be unable to buy the size of holding he wants in one fell swoop. If he's managing a £400 m fund, he wants at least a few million pounds worth of the shares; otherwise the benefit he gets from holding them is going to be so diluted, there's little point to it. Suppose the company he likes is worth £100 m and he wants to put £5 m into it. Five per cent of the company, but only one and a quarter per cent of the fund. And five per cent of the company could represent several weeks or months' worth of normal turnover in that share.

Trying to acquire such a holding quickly would certainly drive the price up against the fund manager. Likewise, in a sale: if his holding represents significantly more than a normal day's turnover in the share, it will often be best not to look for the sale to go through in a single transaction. (It may also happen that at the same time a fund manager wishes to sell, another wants to buy. In this happy situation, it can be possible for each to meet his objectives very quickly.)

Sometimes, the only way to acquire or sell big positions is to do so over a period of weeks. This means that a price or price bracket must be set and kept 'good' for that length of time. Accordingly, the fund manager may give his dealer or broker instructions along the lines of: 'I'd like around three million shares in XYZ Co. Don't pay more than 300p for the moment but keep me in touch.' This might be a sensible instruction to give at a time when the company's share price is 280p.

Or consider: 'I want to get out of my ABC Co shares. I've got

800,000. I see the price is currently 92p. I'm willing to take any-thing above 85p – if the price goes below that, come back to me.'

It is easy to see, therefore, how support and resistance can be set up for shares, especially those of smaller companies where an individual fund manager's actions could account for a lot of the business in the share.

And indeed, *inclined* support and resistance. The dealer charged with selling the 800,000 share parcel may move 200,000 shares on the first day at 90p. Three days later, he moves another 150,000 at 87p. With another 450,000 shares of what the chartists call 'overhead supply' to come and the stockbrokers and market-makers who execute the dealer's sales by now sens-ing it, it is easy to see how the dealer could later be moved to accept 85p, then 84p. (This last deal should not upset the fund manager: his average exit price is still well above the one he orig-inally set.) Here you have 'inclined resistance' – the idea of a sloping line that passes through different prices, and is absolutely central to technical analysis. As we shall now see.

> *'The first two features of a
> graph which most chartists look
> for are the long-term and
> medium-term trends.'*

THE TREND IS YOUR FRIEND
Basic components of any price chart

2

- Charles Dow and the trend
- Short-, medium- and long-term trends
- Bar charts
- Moving averages and the golden cross
- Logarithmic scales

The first two features of a graph which most chartists look for are the long-term and medium-term trends. These are reassuringly easy to grasp, at least when they are set out before you in terms of historical share price graphs. Of course, they are not so easy to spot in real time, but then, there would be no need for technical analysis.

In order to make the basic points about chart components without letting complicated reality get in the way, all the charts in this chapter are happy fictions which make the points clearly. The real world we'll leave until later.

TRENDS

Charles Dow, the editor of the *Wall Street Journal* at the turn of the century, who invented the Dow averages and many of the concepts of charting, considered that the market as a whole was at any time in the grip of three trends: long, medium and short. Long-term trends last for months or years, medium-term trends for weeks to months and short-term ones, for days or possibly a few weeks. In Dow's view, short-term trends were relatively unimportant. He likened the three categories to 'tides, waves and ripples.' Although Dow's area of study was the whole stockmarket and groups of shares within it, his terminology has been adopted by chartists to describe individual shares and individual commodity and currency markets.

Figure 2.1 shows the history of a share price over four years (the Ys along the bottom denote years) and illustrates long-term and medium-term trends.

The share in question has undeniably been 'basically going up' for four years, and therefore its long-term trend is upwards. If the graph were of a share index such as the All-Share, the period would be looked back upon as a bull market.

Obviously, a long-term trend is not a one-way street. It is made up of medium-term trends which will either be in the direction of, or in the opposite direction to, the long-term

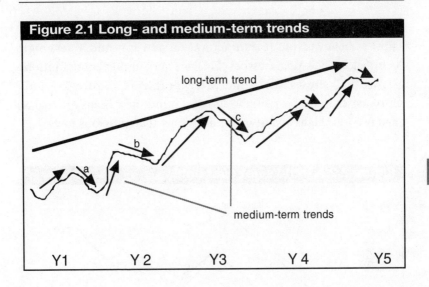

Figure 2.1 Long- and medium-term trends

long-term trend

a
b
c

medium-term trends

Y1 Y 2 Y3 Y 4 Y5

2

trend. The reasons why a share price takes half a step backward for every step forward are straightforward.

There will always be some investors who wish to take advantage of the latest peak by cashing in profits. Correspondingly, in a downtrend, the latest lurch downwards will always make the shares look unbeatably cheap to someone. The fundamentals of the company will change too. Perhaps, looking at Figure 2.1, in the third year, earnings were disappointing, forecasts of which weakened the share price. Another explanation for a reaction against the prevailing trend is that substantial changes in value have to be proven: they are rarely instantaneously recognised by all investors. If buyers believe that a share which was worth 80p last week could be worth 160p by the next time it reports profits, it is not surprising that some holders will feel that's overdoing it. Not everybody reads the same fundamental facts with the same skill or degree of belief: sceptics decide that 120p is fine for them and bring a lot of stock on to the market at that point. So the share's progress up to 160p will rarely be smooth.

There will be periods when it might seem to some holders of

the shares that the long-term trend has reversed. However, the chartist believes that it is intact until a new low and a new high form below their predecessors. This is a very important definition. Figure 2.2 shows the same price graph as Figure 2.1 and emphasises that in a rising long-term trend, new highs are higher than previous highs and new lows are higher than previous lows.

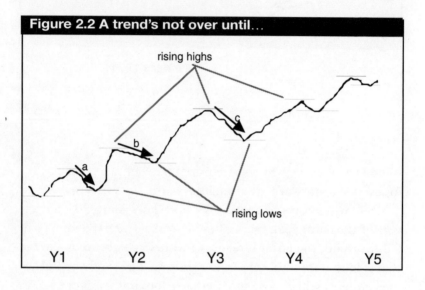

Figure 2.2 A trend's not over until...

rising highs

rising lows

Y1   Y2   Y3   Y4   Y5

Medium-term trends which go against the direction of the long-term trend are known as reactions. Some of these 'reactions' are significant, retracing say around half, perhaps two-thirds (these two amounts – along with several others – are favoured by chartists as expected extents of reactions) of the upwards price movement from the end of the previous reaction. In Figure 2.2, 'a' and 'c' and arguably, 'b' fall into this category.

A significant reaction is known as a 'correction'. In addition to being significant in price terms, corrections also tend to last longer – perhaps for two or three months – than minor reactions, which would be over within a few weeks at the outside. Of course, some 'corrections' turn out to be not medium-term trends within the old long-term trend, but the beginnings of a new long-term trend. These are the ones which form a peak or a low which interrupts the previous pattern of rising highs and rising lows. See Figure 2.3, which is the same price chart as above until the last year, where the different pattern shows that the old long-term rising trend has fairly surely been replaced by a new, falling one.

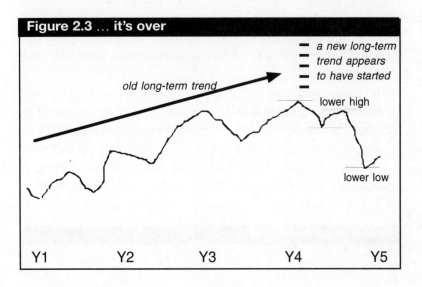

Figure 2.3 ... it's over

a new long-term trend appears to have started

old long-term trend

lower high

lower low

Y1 Y2 Y3 Y4 Y5

It will be apparent that all these features can only be identified in retrospect, and that even then there is room for debate.

The long-term trend could of course as easily be down as up. It could also be sideways, a version sometimes confusingly known as 'trendless'.

A medium-term trend is composed of short-term trends which the chartist analyses in exactly the same way, and using the same terminology as he applies to long- and medium-term trends. Higher highs and higher lows in a medium-term trend mean that it is intact. Similarly, a reaction would appear to be over, once the daily chart showed its own individual pattern of lower highs and lower lows had come to an end.

Whereas chartists believe that there is some predictability about the stockmarket's long- and medium-term trends, there are few who believe the same of its short-term trends. As discussed in Chapter 1, this differentiation does not apply in the commodity and currency markets, where most transactions are designed to reap profit from short-term trends. In the stockmarket, there's comparatively less speculation based on readings of short-term trends alone. However, they are carefully analysed all the same, as the basis for forecasts about their medium- and longer-term cousins.

Obviously, a short-term trend takes less space to depict than a medium- or long-term trend. This means that it is possible to put more information onto the paper or screen. Figures 2.1 to 2.3 simply give a single 'data-point' for each week – the closing share price on each Friday, such as could be taken from a newspaper. When the chartist looks at daily movements in share

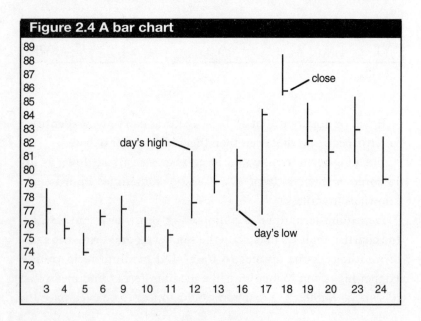

Figure 2.4 A bar chart

prices, to examine the short-term trend, he wants more: at the very least, daily highs and lows in addition to closings. This presentation is shown in Figure 2.4.

This figure deserves a little study by anyone not familiar with this type of graph. It has three data-points for each day. There is no continuous line, although you can imagine where that line would be if this were a more conventional graph by focusing on the tick marks in each vertical bar, which show the price at which the share closed on each day. For instance, on the 10th, it closed at 76p, and that's the price you'd find in the next day's newspapers. But the graph also shows the highest and lowest prices at which shares changed hands during the day – 77p and 75p respectively.

This share shows three short-term trends: up to the 11th, the share moved sideways, then it rallied until the 18th after which it fell. So far, so simple. To the non-chartist, this would simply look like the 'random noise' that you'd get by looking at any share price over a short period. But the chartist can sometimes detect signals in the noise, especially when he has the benefit of three data-points each day. For instance, between the 11th and 12th, there is a 'gap': the lowest price on the 12th was higher than the highest price on the 11th. Another kind of gap can be seen on the 18th: the lowest price on this day is higher than the highest of both the preceding and following days. This is known as an 'island'. It is unusual, and can presage significant price movements. We will return to gaps and islands.

Because of the extra information given by bar charts (you would not be able to detect gaps or islands on a simple line graph such as Figure 2.1), technical analysts prefer to use them even for graphs covering very long periods. Often, the opening price is shown too, usually by mean of a tick on the left hand side of the daily bar. Heaven is four data-points a day.

TREND LINES

Trend lines are the chartist's way of depicting the support and resistance lines described at the end of Chapter 1.

Trend lines are an attempt to define trends: the trend (whether long, medium or short) may be up or down, but is it steep or shallow? Trend lines also help in identification of the end of the trend. There are many ways to draw trend lines but the easiest and by no means the least effective, is with your eyes, a ruler and a pencil.

The basic idea is to connect the danger points in a trend. Thus for a rising trend, the lows dictate the trend line, and in a falling trend, it's the highs (see Figure 2.5). It may seem strange to consider highs as danger points, but remember, the chartist is happy to make money out of any trend, and in a downtrend, he's counting on it continuing to fall. For him, the downtrend's danger points are its highs.

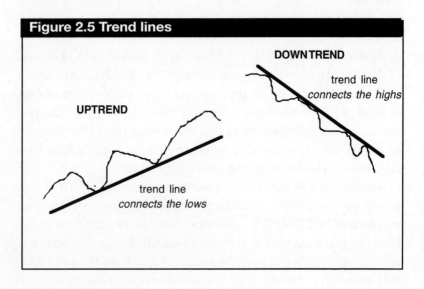

Figure 2.5 Trend lines

DOWNTREND

trend line connects the highs

UPTREND

trend line connects the lows

Once the trend line has been drawn, a lot of chartists, but by no means all, draw a parallel line and fit it as best they can to the highs of their uptrend or lows of their downtrend. This is known as the 'return line' and the space between as the 'trend channel' (see Figure 2.6). For obvious reasons, the upper line in a trend channel is often referred to as the resistance line (or just 'resistance'), and the lower line as the support line ('support').

Figure 2.6 Trend channels

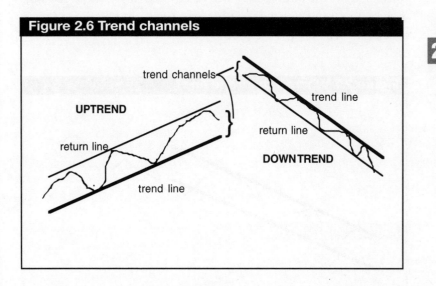

Trend lines are useful to the chartist because they may indicate good times to buy and sell shares. For instance, a share which is in a downtrend and approaching its trend line ('resistance') might be one to sell as the expectation is that the rally which has taken it up to the trendline is about to give way to a price drop. However, a share which pierces its trend line might be about to reverse its trend. Note that these two very similar price 'events' (in both, the price in a downtrend is close to the trend line) lead to opposite outcomes. Such rules by themselves would normally be regarded as too simplistic: they need to be supplemented with other tools from the technical tool kit.

The big problem with trend lines is that they're never in place for long before they need to be reconsidered. As you can draw a straight line between any two points, most chartists look for a third point of contact to confirm the trend line. But this has a niggling habit of being off the straight line given by the other two points. It gets worse when a fourth high or low has to be taken into account. Chartists react to this challenge in different ways: maybe the discrepancy will be ignored, if it's small enough; maybe the trend line will be redrawn. Even chartists joke that a thick pencil can solve the problem (see Figure 2.7).

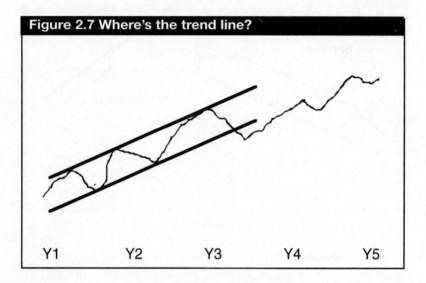

Figure 2.7 Where's the trend line?

In Figure 2.7, the trend line could have been drawn in, as the expectation of where things were going, as soon as the second low was completed halfway through Year 2. Encouragingly, its parallel return line fits not just two but three highs. But by the middle of Year 3, things seems to have got out of kilter. The uptrend itself is still in place (despite the Year 3 low having pierced the trend line), but the trend seems to have slowed down. What now? Where is the true trend line, which is the essential starting point for charting decisions? Take your pick.

Let's assume that the chartists are considering the graph in Figure 2.7 at the beginning of Year 5 with a view to analysing what's going to happen in Year 6. One response is to try to find new a new trend line which fits all the price history under consideration reasonably well, as in Figure 2.8.

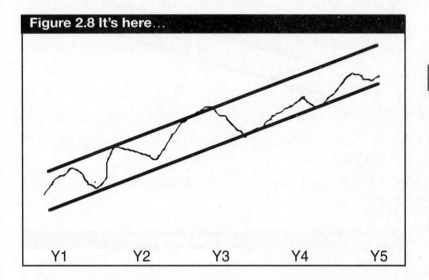

Figure 2.8 It's here...

Y1   Y2   Y3   Y4   Y5

Hey presto – the trend's intact! Possibly this chartist has spotted an earlier low, a year or two before this graph starts, which gives him confidence that the trend lines should be shallower than those in Figure 2.7. Alternatively, he may not be so rigorous about the number of points of contact.

Or he might decide that it's time to redraw the long-term trend, recognising the fact that it is no longer as strong as it was: see Figure 2.9.

The little bulge over the new resistance line late in Year 2 could be explained away by 'materiality': a view that an exception of, say, 4 or 5 per cent is insufficient to disqualify the analysis.

A variation on the same theme is to suggest that whereas the trend line previously provided support for the share price, its role has now switched to acting as resistance. This is a popular concept in charting: see Figure 2.10.

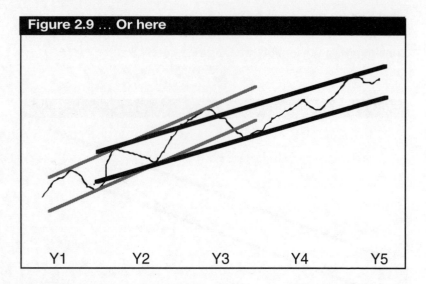

Figure 2.9 … Or here

Y1   Y2   Y3   Y4   Y5

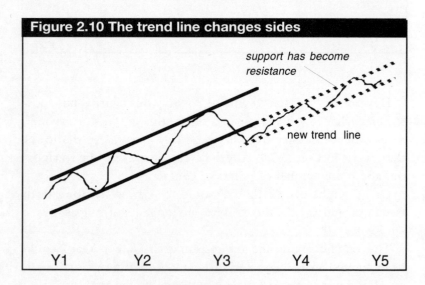

Figure 2.10 The trend line changes sides

support has become
resistance

new trend line

Y1   Y2   Y3   Y4   Y5

At this point, you could be either exasperated or thrilled. There are endless ways to interpret the same chart. Some chartists are flexible and would respond to this chart with one or other of the interpretations given in Figures 2.8 to 2.10. Others might consider that the message just wasn't clear enough to make it the basis of an investment decision. However, almost all would agree that the long-term trend was still in place. Sceptics see the scope for debate about where trend lines should be drawn as a central weakness of charting. This is unfair. No profession exists without argument within it about what its general principles are, and how they should be applied to specific cases. Why should technical analysis be any different?

Medium- and short-term trends may be analysed in precisely the same way as long-term trends. To get the idea, just imagine that each of the graphs shown in Figures 2.1 to 2.10 has months along the bottom instead of years. You could be analysing what happened to the five-year graph in the last four months of Year 2, say. What have been discussed as highs and lows between medium-term trends would be turned into highs and lows between short-term trends, with the same arguments about which were the right trend lines.

In the commodities and futures markets, with their unvarying usage of three or four price points each day (or period: it's not unusual for traders here to be working with five-minute intervals along the bottom of their graphs), the difficulty of ill-fitting trend lines is considerable. With just one price point per period, the problem is limited. But if you are using high, low and closing prices, then although the close is above your uptrend line, the low might not be. See Figure 2.11.

Most short-term traders prefer their trend lines not to cross over any 'price action' including intra-day prices (i.e., highs and lows) and would prefer the lower of the two trend lines shown. An alternative approach is to disregard any highs or lows that do not genuinely stand out. For instance, a high which warrants inclusion in a downtrend must be the highest price for 10 days (five days before, and five days after the day it was recorded). If you inspect Figure 2.11 carefully, you will see that there is no price which stands out on this basis. The low on the fifth might count,

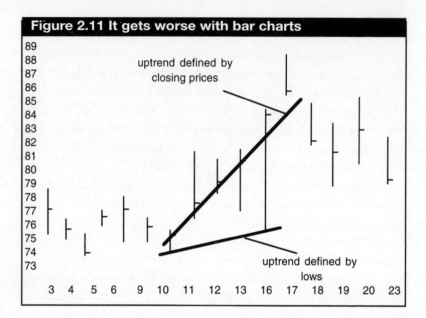

Figure 2.11 It gets worse with bar charts

depending on what happened on the two business days before the start of the graph. Similarly, the high on the 18th might count, as long as it wasn't superseded by a higher high on the next business day. A further school of thought contends that, in the short-term markets, extreme highs and lows are aberrations, and should not be taken as indicative of the market's mainstream trend.

On the problem of defining trend lines, chartists fall into one of two categories. Some argue that a rule is a rule: if the chart won't yield up a decent trend line according to a precise formula, then forget it and look at another chart (for another share, another commodity). Others are pragmatic. But both would probably urge you to 'see what works for you.'

MOVING AVERAGES

Moving averages define trend lines without resort to the eye, ruler and pencil. But they don't make the job any easier.

A moving average is an average of the last so many days' share prices. Each day, it is updated by dropping the earliest price used for the previous day's calculation, and adding the latest price – hence it is a 'moving' average. You can use five, ten, 200 or any other number of days.

2

Example

Suppose ClevaNuShops comes to the market on Monday, 1 February, and records the prices shown in Figure 2.12.

Figure 2.12 ClevaNuShops: closing prices							
1st	140p	8th	160p	15th	160p	22nd	170p
2nd	145p	9th	158p	16th	165p	23rd	170p
3rd	147p	10th	155p	17th	162p	24th	162p
4th	148p	11th	157p	18th	167p	25th	160p
5th	155p	12th	159p	19th	170p	26th	155p

To work out a five-day moving average, add up the prices for the first five days and divide by five. That's 735p divided by five, which equals 147p – the average price for the week ending 5 February. This is the first five-day average price you can work out, as you don't have prices prior to the 1st. On the 9th, you can look up the closing price on the 8th and add it to the closing prices for the 2nd to the 5th. That comes to 755p. Divide by 5 again and you'll get 151p. And so on. Figure 2.13 gives five- and ten-day moving average share prices for ClevaNuShops. The principle is identical for any other period. Obviously, it helps to have a computer if you do this often.

Moving averages smooth out share price movements. The longer the period over which the moving average is calculated, the smoother the result. You can appreciate this readily from Figure 2.14, which plots the figures given in Figure 2.13.

Figure 2.13 ClevaNuShops: five- and ten-day moving average share prices

date	5-day moving average	10-day moving average
8th	147p	
9th	151p	
10th	154p	
11th	155p	
12th	157p	
15th	158p	152p
16th	158p	154p
17th	159p	156p
18th	161p	158p
19th	163p	160p
22nd	165p	161p
23rd	167p	162p
24th	168p	164p
25th	164p	164p
26th	166p	165p

Figure 2.14 Moving averages

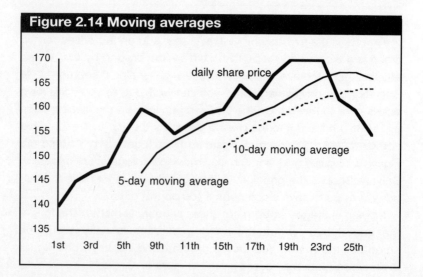

The five-day average doesn't have any of the highs and lows of the daily prices, and the 10-day average is smoother still. See how the daily price falls back sharply in the last three days of the month. The five-day average just catches a hint of this. The ten-day average merely levels off: it doesn't fall at all (although it will, in early March).

At first sight, it may seem that the moving average is a wonderful way of sorting out serious price movements from background noise. This will tell you what's a minor reaction, and what's a true correction! If only it were that simple.

A 'buy signal' often quoted by chartists is that the moving average is just beginning to rise in response to a continuing strengthening in the daily share price. This could be an indication that a downtrend is reversing. Consider Figure 2.15, which shows ClevaNuShops' weekly closing prices and a ten-week moving average for a first full year.

Figure 2.15 A single moving average...

An investor reading *the share price alone* for signs of a rise might have made a move in June, and found himself disappointed within the month. But had he consulted the moving average, he wouldn't have bought shares until October, because only then did it move up, signalling that the 'price is off the bottom.' Yes, in this case, whoever bought in June would eventually have had their rewards, and bigger ones too, since they bought in at a lower price. But the chartist, don't forget, looks for his rewards at least to begin to show in the short term.

Some will want to point out that the October rally in the share price could have failed to follow through, and still the ten-week average would have given a 'buy' signal. Figure 2.16 shows the same graph, with just the November and December figures revised.

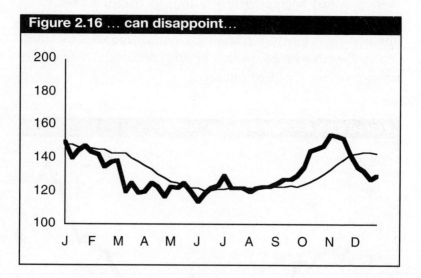

Figure 2.16 ... can disappoint...

Here, the moving average gives the same 'buy' signal, but its follower is confounded by the downturn after October. Assuming he thought the signs were sufficiently positive in mid October, he would have bought the shares at around 147p, and things would have looked good for the first fortnight. But that nasty downturn in November takes him by surprise. His stop-loss order will save him from taking a bath, but all the same, it's a disappointing trade.

There are several answers to this problem, the first of which is to use two moving averages. A typical combination used in the stockmarket is ten and 40 weeks. Figure 2.17 is the same graph as Figure 2.16, this time showing a 40-week moving average too.

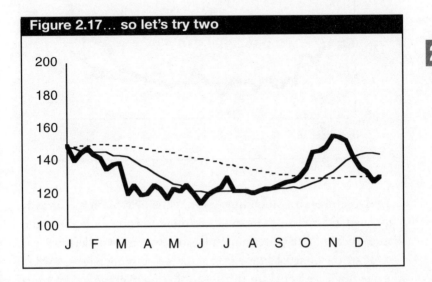

Figure 2.17... so let's try two

Here, even by the end of December, the second, slower-to-adjust, moving average has barely registered the share's recovery since August. It certainly does not give a 'buy' signal. It's easy to appreciate how using two averages together will improve the quality of chart signals. The number of shares demonstrating sustained price rises is many fewer than those which experience temporary ones.

We can also see how the two averages together would have worked, assuming the autumn price rise had followed through into November and December. Figure 2.18 replicates Figure 2.15, superimposing a 40-week moving average.

In this case, the 40-week average does rise and confirm the 'buy' signal given by the ten-week average, but not conclusively until

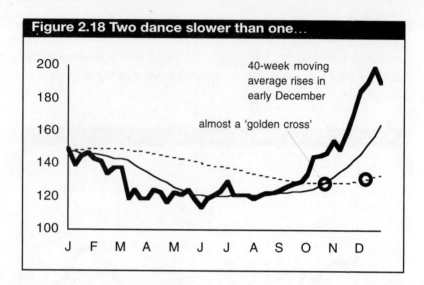

Figure 2.18 Two dance slower than one...

early December, by which time a lot of the price gain has already happened. Of course, there might be more to come in January and February, but on this occasion, it has not worked wonderfully.

One of the chartist's favourite signals is a 'golden cross', when the short average cuts up through the long average, *which must itself also be moving upwards*. Figure 2.18 just fails the second half of this test: the long average does not move up until later. Clearly, whilst the long average can help the chartist avoid false signals, the extra wait as compared with just using a short average can cost him some of the gains he would have made when the short average acts reliably. There are many recipes for quickening it up, without sacrificing the principle. One way is to give bigger weightings to the more recent prices in the 40-week series. Compare Figure 2.19 with 2.18.

You will see that the 40-week moving average is now more responsive to ClevaNuShops' autumn price rally. You might almost say it was a better indicator. Don't be grudging: in this case, there's no doubt about it. The crossover of the two moving averages is now a genuine golden cross as the longer one is already rising when the short one comes up through it. This

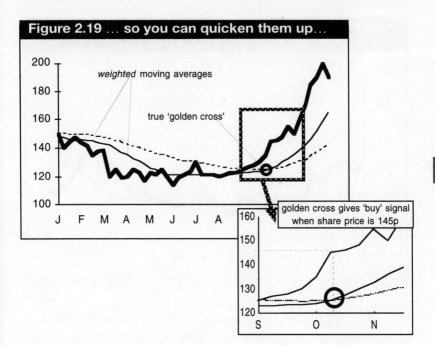

Figure 2.19 ... so you can quicken them up...

weighted moving averages

true 'golden cross'

golden cross gives 'buy' signal when share price is 145p

2

gives you a firm 'buy' signal in early October, setting you up for a handsome profit by putting you into the shares at 145p.

How was this achieved? By simple mathematics. The last ten prices in the 40-week moving average were multiplied by 7.5, the preceding ten by 5 and the ten before that by 2.5. The earliest ten prices were left unchanged. After adding up the results, the total was divided by 160 instead of 40 (because 10×7.5 plus 10×5 plus 10×2.5 plus 10×1 adds up to 160). The effect of this is to make the 40-week average give greater weight to the most recent prices and less to the earlier ones.

This even works tolerably if we change the prices back again so that the autumn rally is reversed in the last two months. The early October golden cross signals a buy at 145p, allowing you to close out above 150p as the rally falters three weeks later: the signal gets you into the shares early enough for the trade to meet its costs. This may seem no great victory to the sceptic, but it is as valuable to the chartist to exit from loss-making situations

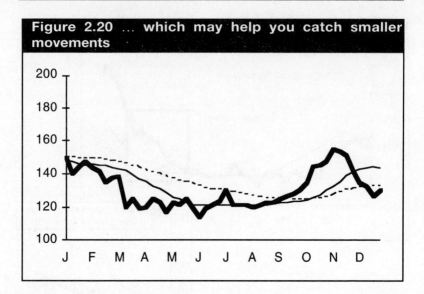

Figure 2.20 ... which may help you catch smaller movements

still wearing his shirt, as it is to make a profit. As Sam Bass, a great speculator, is rumoured to have replied to the question, 'How do you make money?', 'Don't lose any.'

But don't get carried away. There's no magic about weighted moving averages. This one was cooked up to order to make a point. It worked here, but there's no saying it will work on the next share you are thinking of buying. It's always possible to jiggle the formula to create what would have been successful 'buy' signals from historic charts. Real life is more challenging.

The general rule that two moving averages are better than one is worth remembering, but you should also remember that sometimes four and ten-week averages work, sometimes five- and 40-week, and sometimes, two- and seven-day. Brian Marber, a respected UK chartist, uses 63- and 253-day averages (three months and one year). Sometimes weighted moving averages help. In fact, you could probably demonstrate that they always did, as long as you were prepared to jiggle the weighting formula – for instance, give double, triple or quintuple weighting to the latest half, quarter or tenth of the prices – for every chart you saw. Chartists use limitless variations on this theme, including the exponential moving average, which uses all previous prices. And then they go on to use an equally diverse list of secondary indicators to confirm the primary ones. All formulae work some of the time. None works all of the time.

As the chartists say about trend line definitions, you have to find out what works for you. If that sounds disingenuous, don't try charting.

2

SCALES

As has already been said, the horizontal scale in a share price graph can be marked out in anything from centuries to seconds, as long as you have the past prices.

Charts of share prices going back to the early 1800s make interesting viewing as they always go reassuringly upwards. This is only partly because chart-makers aren't generally interested in shares which are no longer around because the companies went bust. It's a fact that shares as a whole have always been an excellent investment over the very long term (see, for instance *Stocks for the Long Run*, which is listed in **Further Reading** on page 237). However, few of the readers of this book are doing so to develop their expertise in century-long trends, or even decade-long ones.

Five or ten years of share price history is ample to arrive at a charting conclusion, and if you're interested in very short-term investments – a few months at the outside, you'll pay most attention to the very recent record.

Unless you have some inside information and don't mind the risk of being prosecuted, the stockmarket is not really the place for very short-term trading: aiming to make a profit within days rather than weeks. Therefore few stockmarket chartists look at intra-day prices in any more detail than the open, high, low, close format. Stockmarkets just don't see the volume of trading that makes the study of, say, 15-minute or hourly price movements worth the trouble. This is not true of the FT-SE 100 Index, which is watched and traded on such a basis, but that is a creature of the financial futures markets, not the Stock Exchange.

Intra-day trading on the financial futures, commodity and currency markets is the province of the professional. The very least you'll need is a Reuters screen, a thick wallet, iron discipline and a lot more knowledge than this book can provide. Most small investors who get into this area are reckoned to get out again, minus their money, within a year.

This book looks at horizontal scales which are divided into days, years or points in between.

Which brings us to vertical scales. You need to understand what a logarithmic scale is to be a chartist. Fortunately, this does not involve dredging up your O-level knowledge about log tables.

A log scale puts things in proportion. For instance, if you bought ClevaNuShops shares at 140p, held them for two years and sold at 280p (let's say the rally continued after all), you've made 140p. You did well, but so did the person you sold them to. He held them for just six months and sold at 420p. In other

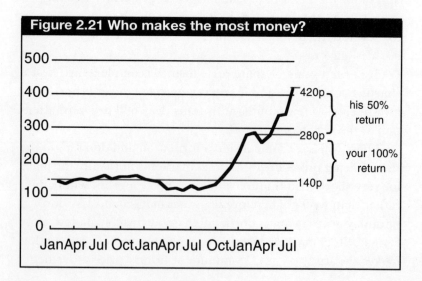

Figure 2.21 Who makes the most money?

words, he made 140p too. Who made the most money? Neither of you – you both made the same amount. But somehow, you know you did better than him?

You did: you doubled your money, for a 100 per cent return (140p profit on a 140p investment: 140 divided by 140 = 1, or 100 per cent). He made only a 50 per cent return (140p profit on a 280p investment: 140/280 = 0.5, or 50 per cent). You did twice as well as him, although he got his return in quarter of the time, which probably puts him ahead on points.

A log scale gets this over. Figure 2.21 shows all the information on a normal graph.

Now consider the same information presented on a log scale graph, where the prices are bunched closer together as they get higher (Figure 2.22).

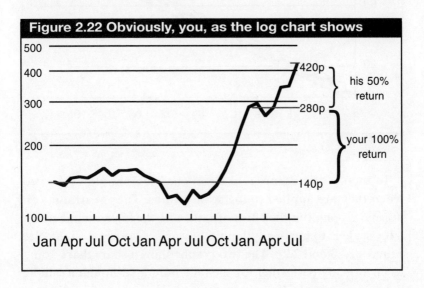

Figure 2.22 Obviously, you, as the log chart shows

A log scale gives as much attention to the percentage change as to the absolute figures themselves.

Log scales put big price movements – of say 100 per cent or more – into perspective. In Figures 2.21 and 2.22, the

ClevaNuShops price rises by 270 per cent from its low point to its high. Not many shares do this in such a short period. When you're dealing with one that does, it's as well to look at it on a log scale. But, over the space of a few years, many share prices move by this order of magnitude, so long-run prices are often presented in log scale form.

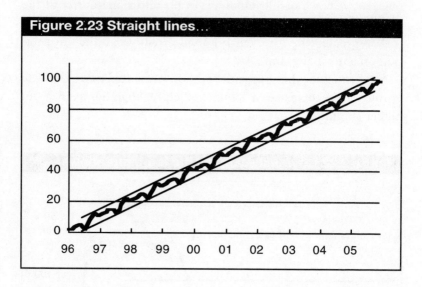

Figure 2.23 Straight lines...

In theory, trend lines and trend channels should be curved when they are applied to log scale graphs. They're straight on normal graphs, but the effect of bunching the higher numbers on a log scale is to curve anything that was previously straight. See Figures 2.23 and 2.24. The two graphs show a share that's going to be a steady performer for the millennium, although it will be best to get in early. If you inspect them closely, you'll agree that they're the same share. In Figure 2.23, a clear long-term trend channel is evident which isn't going to need any revisions for years. But look what's happened to it in Figure 2.24.

For unexplained reasons, chartists who use log scales draw straight trend lines on them. Of course, they revise them often, too.

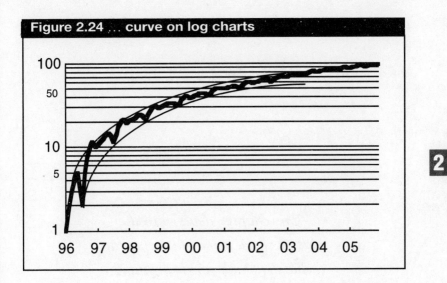

Figure 2.24 ... curve on log charts

'This chapter deals with the classic share price patterns that chartists look for as primary indicators of what's going to happen next.'

THE HEAD AND SHOULDERS AND FRIENDS

- Patterns which say ...
- ... 'It should start to rise'
- ... 'It should start to fall'
- ... 'It will carry on in the same direction'
- and words of warning

This chapter deals with the classic share price patterns that chartists look for as primary indicators of what's going to happen next. Most investors have heard of these, even if they are ignorant about what they look like and mean.

The patterns fall into two categories. 'Reversal' patterns, in theory, denote a change of trend – lows which denote the start of an uptrend, and highs which say, 'that's it, folks.' If you spot one of these, you may expect that a new trend, in the opposite direction to what has gone before, will now commence. The patterns for highs are identical to those for lows, except turned on their heads. Thus, the 'head and shoulders' which tops off an upwards run in the share price corresponds to the 'inverse head and shoulders' which would form a bottom after a downwards movement in the share price, indicating that now, at least part of the fall should be retraced.

'Continuation' patterns occur during a pause in a trend, and indicate that it will continue in the same direction as before.

In addition to the basic 'direction-pointing' functions of these patterns, most chartists suggest that close examination of them will enable an estimate to be made of how far the new or continued trend will go.

Modern reversal and continuation patterns are all two-dimensional, in the sense that a shape of some sort can be drawn around them. Charles Dow and his followers in the 1920s and 1930s also identified patterns that had forecasting power, although they defined them as single dimensional lines. In *The Dow Theory*, Robert Rhea defined a line as:

' ... a price movement extending two to three weeks or longer, during which period the price variation ... moves within a range of approximately 5 per cent. Such a movement indicates either accumulation or distribution ... Advances above the 'line' ... predict higher prices; ... conversely ... declines below the 'line' imply ... lower prices ... Inferences drawn from one day's movement ... are of but little value except when 'lines' are being drawn...'

Rhea was in fact discussing the simultaneous movements of the two Dow Averages (Industrial and Transportation), but his thinking gave an early lead to the theories discussed in this chapter.

WORDS OF WARNING ON THE CLASSIC PATTERNS

1 Reversal patterns – i.e., any share price pattern that marks the end of one trend and the beginning of the next – won't in fact get you out at the top or in at the bottom. For that, you need pure luck. The reason is that you can't see any of these patterns until they're complete, and that means the share price has already reversed. *You can see only these patterns in retrospect.* What these patterns do accomplish, in theory at any rate, is to put you into the new trend, safe in the knowledge – or trust – that the reversal has happened and the next one should be a whole trend away.

3

2 It helps a lot if there's something to reverse. Don't waste time trying to detect these patterns emerging from the end of a trendless share price graph. Instead, look for a share which the market has built into, as Burton Malkiel (no chartist, he) puts it, a 'castle in the air,' or one whose bombing-out has gone on for so long

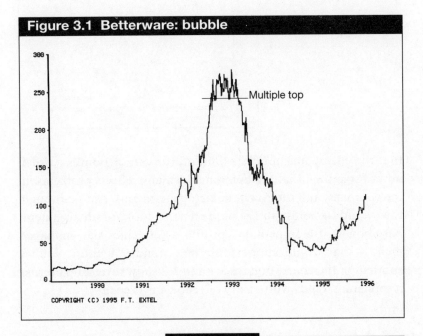

Figure 3.1 Betterware: bubble

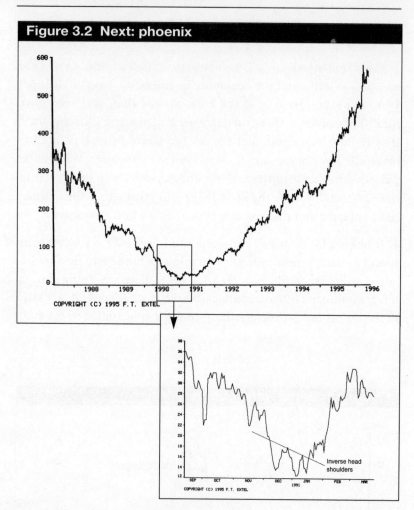

Figure 3.2 Next: phoenix

that the enemy has, in all likelihood, run out of bombs (whilst never forgetting, that the bombing normally reflects problems in the company, and these can, in fact, be terminal). And, although this would be heresy to the pure chartist, look for an argument based on the fundamentals – profits, asset values, new management – that would support the new trend you think you've spotted on the chart. Figures 3.1 and 3.2 show reversal patterns, terminating trends with plenty of scope for reversal.

3 When you're looking for these patterns, don't look too hard: THEY SHOULD LEAP OUT AT YOU! If they don't, then move on to another chart. It's a useful aspect of charting that it allows you to screen lots of shares in a short time.

4 The patterns do not occur frequently. In Chapter 9, where there are charts for most of the UK's top 25 shares for the period from October 1995 to April 1996 – that's 12 years of share price history in all – there are few definitive examples. This is why most of the day-to-day commentary put out by stock-market chartists uses the terms defined in this chapter sparingly.

5 When they do occur, they're rarely perfect. Look at one carefully and ask yourself at which point you would have been able to act upon it as a buy signal. How many false starts were there? How many of the preceding squiggles in the line would have looked like 'buy' or 'sell' signals at the time, and turned out to be false?

If you had got in when the formation was complete, how much money would you have made subsequently? Enough for all the studying and waiting to be worth it? Don't kid yourself into thinking that you would have sold out at the high. On the way to that high are numerous corrections. Would you really have held on through these? If so, why wouldn't you then have held on through the high. What was it that – on the day – made it so different from all the other highs that preceded it? How much of your profit would you have given back to the market before you indeed read it as the high? *Ask yourself, how much you really might have made.* You're unlikely to give yourself the right answers, but you should ask these questions nonetheless, because they're the ones you'll encounter when you try technical analysis in real life.

6 Take note that the patterns which supposedly denote reversals can occur at other times too: see Figure 3.3. Figure 3.3, you will note, is part of the graph shown in Figure 3.2. In the earlier chart, the reversal is marked by a clear head and shoulders. But look more closely at Next's amazing run down to that final

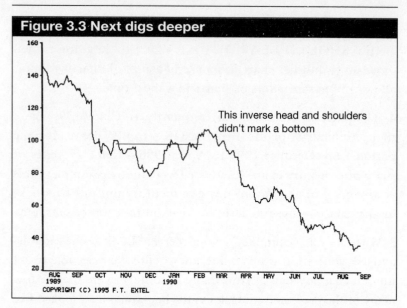

Figure 3.3 Next digs deeper

This inverse head and shoulders didn't mark a bottom

COPYRIGHT (C) 1995 F.T. EXTEL

definitive reversal. You'll see several other inverse head and shoulders on the way, including this one in Figure 3.3. Each one is a failed reversal signal.

7 The extent of and time taken to form the previous trend and the formation itself should be considered. These patterns can be seen on daily, weekly and five-year charts. One that has built up over several months and can be discerned on a multi-year chart showing just weekly prices is considered to be more significant and reliable than a baby version that can be seen on a daily chart.

8 Always examine carefully the value scale (the vertical one) of the graph you are considering. Charts are normally computer-generated and graphing programs customarily work out how to present the data *so as to fill the space available*. For instance, if the share price has joggled along between 180p and 200p, the scale is likely to start at 170p and end at 210p (see Figure 3.4, middle graph). This enables you to read the graph much more accurately than if the value scale went from 0p to 210p (see Figure 3.4, top graph), in which case the same line would simply be a gentle undulation running along the top.

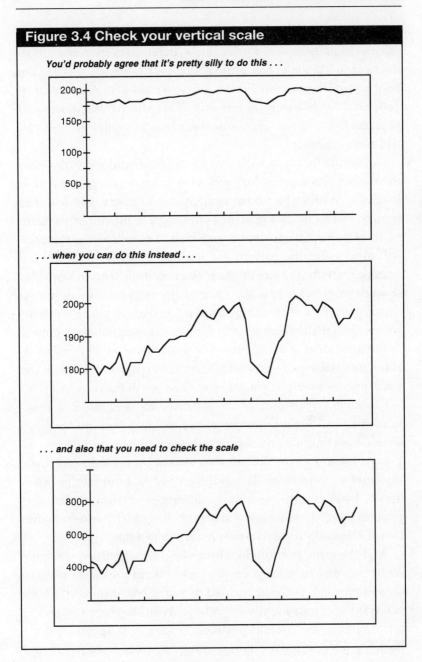

Figure 3.4 Check your vertical scale

You'd probably agree that it's pretty silly to do this . . .

. . . when you can do this instead . . .

. . . and also that you need to check the scale

The trap you can fall into, if you don't read the scale carefully, is to assume that a price line which moves from the top to the bottom of the graph presents useful trading opportunities. In the middle graph in Figure 3.4, it would not. A move from 180p to 200p is barely 11 per cent. Take out dealing costs and your margin of error for timing on getting in and out, and you will surely agree.

Carry this thinking with you when you examine the patterns themselves. As a rule of thumb, look for reversal patterns that involve a comfortable 10 per cent change in prices – for instance from the neckline of a head and shoulders to the top of its head. Most patterns are associated with targets as to how far the price will move after the pattern has been completed. Typically the target equates to the size of the formation itself. Thus a head and shoulders spread over a 20p span of the vertical scale should in theory be followed by a 20p fall in price. This could be a worthwhile signal if the share price is 80p – as the percentage change is 25 per cent. If that works, you will make some money out of it. But if the share price was 380p, then the expected 20p fall in the share price is worth only 5 per cent – not worth the risks involved.

Careful interpretation of the vertical scale is especially important when reading a share manual which gives a graph for every share. Nestling alongside a graph such as the middle one in Figure 3.4 you might find another with a totally different scale, say from 400p to 800p. The graphs could *look* similar, but they aren't. Work out the percentage difference between the highest price used on the scale and the lowest: 200p is 18 per cent higher than 170p; 800p is 100 per cent higher than 400p.

And the same caution, in a lower key, also applies to the time scale. Is it measured in years or weeks? What looks like a sharp movement on a graph measured in years, could in reality have taken three or four months to roll out. With the chartist typically looking for a short-term payback, what might appear to have been a golden opportunity might in practice have been just too long and drawn-out to bear.

REVERSAL PATTERNS – TOPS

There's no question about it. The most effective way to make a fortune in the investment markets is to spot the change of trend. To get in at the bottom and out at the top. And no medium gets this idea over better than a chart. Whoever looked at a share price chart containing any respectable mixture of peaks and troughs, and did not think, however fleetingly, about what they could have made by buying when it was bombed out and selling when it had become a castle in the air.

You don't have to be a chartist to buy this proposition. Even Warren 'We will never sell this holding' Buffett looks out for bottoms. His greatest coups, including his investments in American Express (the first one, in the 1960s), the Washington Post and GEICO, all involved spotting the bottom, even if in the latter two cases, he wasn't interested in cashing in at the tops. Buffett, of course, doesn't identify a bottom by analysing share price patterns. But the chartist does.

A game less often played, but equally effective, is to sell at the top and buy back at the bottom. For reasons already described, this involves limitations which do not apply to the investor expecting a share price to rise. However, not so many that the amateur chartist can't, if he thinks he's spotted a real top, back his judgement by buying a put option.

On the next few pages is a series of figures which exemplify the most commonly quoted identifiable patterns which, *when they form after an uptrend*, are said to denote that a downtrend should follow.

Customarily, books on technical analysis accompany their accounts of these famous patterns with descriptions of what's happening in the minds of investors as the patterns are carved out, along the lines of '... investors expected support at this level, having seen it before, are now shocked that it does not occur... the market argument now moves over to the bears...' Here we will dispense with that. Even if accurate, such descriptions are neither here nor there: the fact is these patterns are supposed to tell you a trend is over.

The main patterns are:

- **head and shoulders** (see Figures 3.5 to 3.7): most chartists suggest that the head and shoulders pattern is (a) 'reliable', meaning that on a good fraction of occasions, its occurrence is indeed followed by a fall in price, and (b) frequent.
- **double top** (see Figure 3.8);
- **triple top** (see Figure 3.9);
- **saucer top** (see Figure 3.10) the saucer is inverted – it looks like a shallow hill;
- **descending triangle** (see Figure 3.11);
- **V** (again, inverted: see Figure 3.12).

The six patterns above normally form over the course of a few weeks, quite possibly months. The three below would typically form within a day or two. They may well be part of one of the first six and if so, would be seen as emphasising the message given by the larger pattern:

- **spike** (see Figure 3.12);
- **island top** (see Figure 3.13);
- **key reversal** (see Figure 3.14).

Figure 3.5 Head and shoulders

Possibly the chartist's favourite indicator. It comprises five phases.

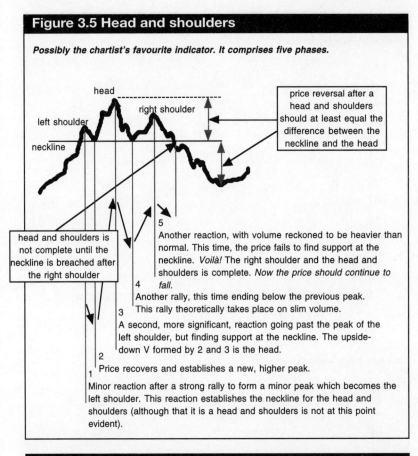

price reversal after a head and shoulders should at least equal the difference between the neckline and the head

head and shoulders is not complete until the neckline is breached after the right shoulder

5 Another reaction, with volume reckoned to be heavier than normal. This time, the price fails to find support at the neckline. *Voilà!* The right shoulder and the head and shoulders is complete. *Now the price should continue to fall.*

4 Another rally, this time ending below the previous peak. This rally theoretically takes place on slim volume.

3 A second, more significant, reaction going past the peak of the left shoulder, but finding support at the neckline. The upside-down V formed by 2 and 3 is the head.

2 Price recovers and establishes a new, higher peak.

1 Minor reaction after a strong rally to form a minor peak which becomes the left shoulder. This reaction establishes the neckline for the head and shoulders (although that it is a head and shoulders is not at this point evident).

Figure 3.6 Head and shoulders with rising neckline

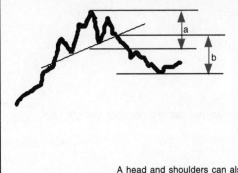

The price objective after the right shoulder has been completed remains the difference between the top of the head and the neckline directly below (a). This should be measured from the point where the neckline is breached by the right shoulder (b).

A head and shoulders can also demonstrate a falling neckline.

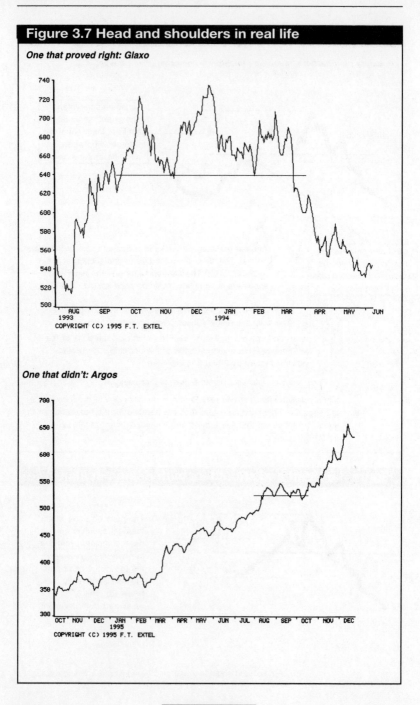

Figure 3.7 Head and shoulders in real life

One that proved right: Glaxo

COPYRIGHT (C) 1995 F.T. EXTEL

One that didn't: Argos

COPYRIGHT (C) 1995 F.T. EXTEL

Figure 3.8 Double top

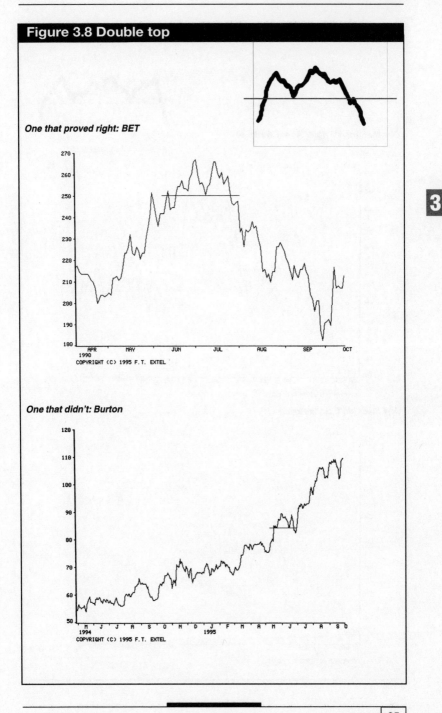

One that proved right: BET

One that didn't: Burton

Figure 3.9 Triple top

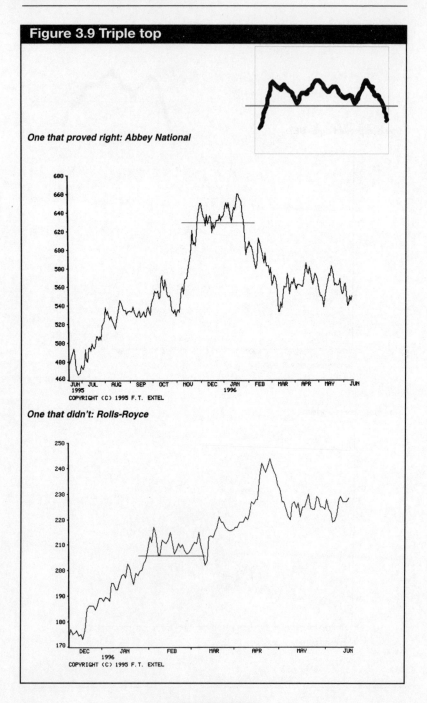

One that proved right: Abbey National

COPYRIGHT (C) 1995 F.T. EXTEL

One that didn't: Rolls-Royce

COPYRIGHT (C) 1995 F.T. EXTEL

Figure 3.10 Saucer top

... also known as a rounded top

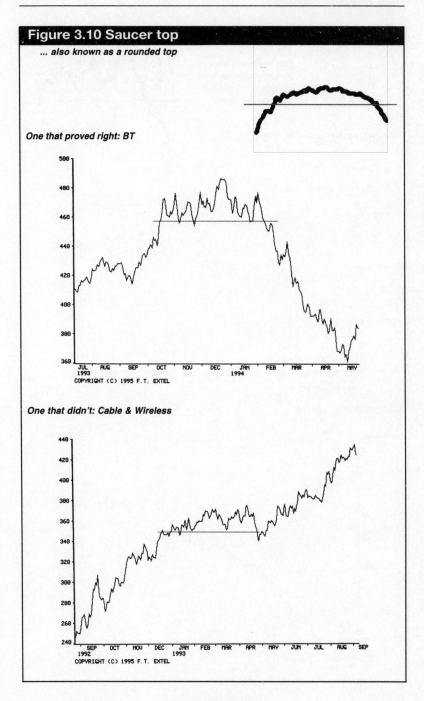

One that proved right: BT

COPYRIGHT (C) 1995 F.T. EXTEL

One that didn't: Cable & Wireless

COPYRIGHT (C) 1995 F.T. EXTEL

3

Figure 3.11 Descending triangle

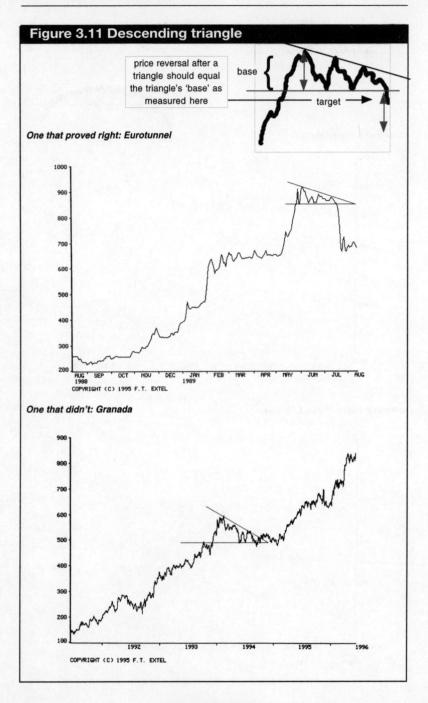

price reversal after a triangle should equal the triangle's 'base' as measured here

base

target

One that proved right: Eurotunnel

COPYRIGHT (C) 1995 F.T. EXTEL

One that didn't: Granada

COPYRIGHT (C) 1995 F.T. EXTEL

68

Figure 3.12 Vs and spikes

These are two separate patterns. A spike occurs over a few days at most. The V could be a few weeks in the making. A V isn't necessarily accompanied by a spike

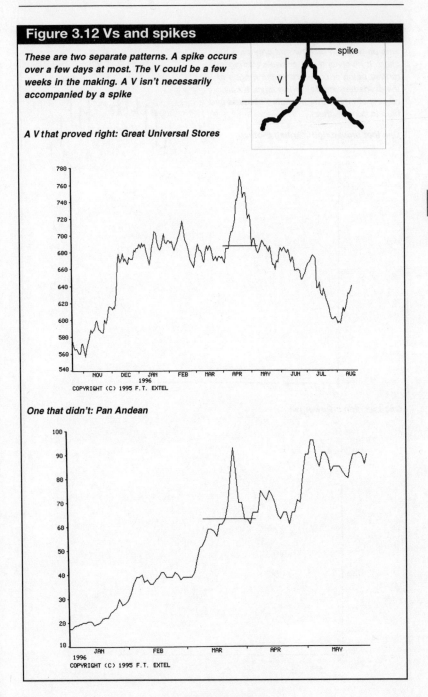

A V that proved right: Great Universal Stores

COPYRIGHT (C) 1995 F.T. EXTEL

One that didn't: Pan Andean

COPYRIGHT (C) 1995 F.T. EXTEL

Figure 3.13 Island top

This pattern can be detected only on a bar chart. It involves a day or two's trading ranges being entirely above the ranges of the preceding and following days. It can be part of one of the preceding patterns and help to confirm them.

One that proved right: British Biotech

One that didn't: Powergen

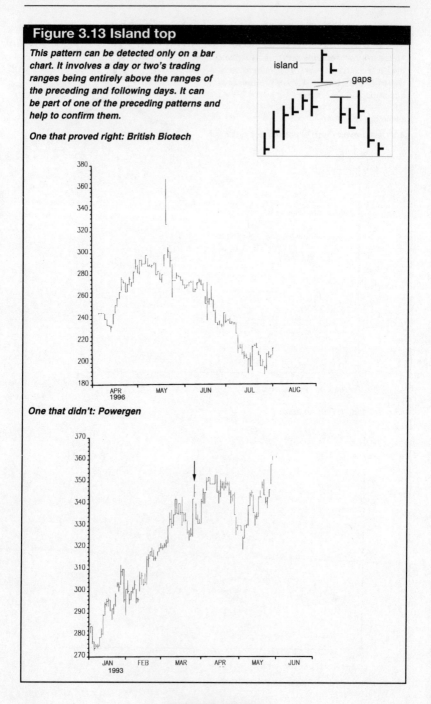

Figure 3.14 Key reversal

Another bar chart-only pattern. After a 'good run' in one direction or another, the trend is sharply reversed by a wide-ranging day's trading which sees (in a bearish key reversal) (1) a new intra-day high, (2) an intra-day low which is lower than for several days past and (3) a closing price at or close to the day's low. Prices may now be expected to continue to fall away for several days.

One that proved right: GKN

One that didn't: National Westminster

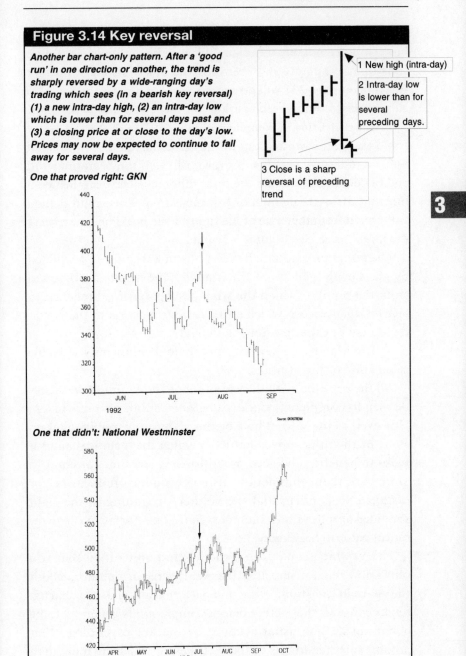

Many of the formations described on the preceding pages have variants, notably the 'diamond' and the 'multiple top' (more tops than a triple top). Several of the books listed in **Further Reading** on page 237 will give you a more complete rundown on sub-species, although each author has favourites and blind spots.

The target price movement following a V, a double or triple top or saucer is worked out in the same way as that for a head and shoulders. A neckline is drawn through the beginning and end of the formation and the price difference between the neckline and the extreme high or low measured. This result is then subtracted from the price at the right of the neckline, to arrive at the target price. See Figures 3.5. and 3.6

The target price after a breakout from a triangle is calculated by measuring the base of the triangle. The result is subtracted from the point at which the triangular pattern is breached to give a target price at which a first serious reaction to the downtrend may be expected. See Figure 3.11.

Spikes, islands and key reversals do not lend themselves to the calculation of target prices.

All the patterns, with the exception of the V, should in theory be seen to complete themselves before trading action is taken. However, as the second half of the pattern invariably takes up some of the price movement from which the technical analyst seeks to benefit, advanced practitioners sometimes attempt to anticipate their completion, using secondary indicators, for instance, to confirm that the volume of trading in the right shoulder of a head and shoulders indeed conforms to the theoretical pattern. See Figure 3.5.

The V, which equates to a sudden and unjustified (but you only know that for sure after the event) surge of optimism about the share in question, is the one pattern for which the chartist might consider that acting before completion is generally to be encouraged. The usual account of market psychology that accompanies renditions of the V strikes me as having more than a grain of truth about it. The first, upside, half of the V (or the downside half in a V marking a bottom) is reckoned to be especially important if it occurs on high volume. In this event, so the chartists' account goes, a lot of shares have changed hands and more or less everyone who wanted to be 'in' is in. They share ownership of the company with fellow shareholders who, in this case, are all sitting on a handsome profit. Outside, are very few buyers. It wouldn't be difficult for these ingredients to turn into a share price rout.

REVERSAL PATTERNS – BOTTOMS

The bottom formations are simply the mirror images of the top formations:

- **inverse head and shoulders** (see Figure 3.15);
- **double bottom**;
- **triple bottom**;
- **saucer** (this time the saucer is the right way up);
- **ascending triangle** (see Figure 3.16);
- **V** (right way up);
- **spike**;
- **island bottom**.

Figure 3.15 Inverse head and shoulders

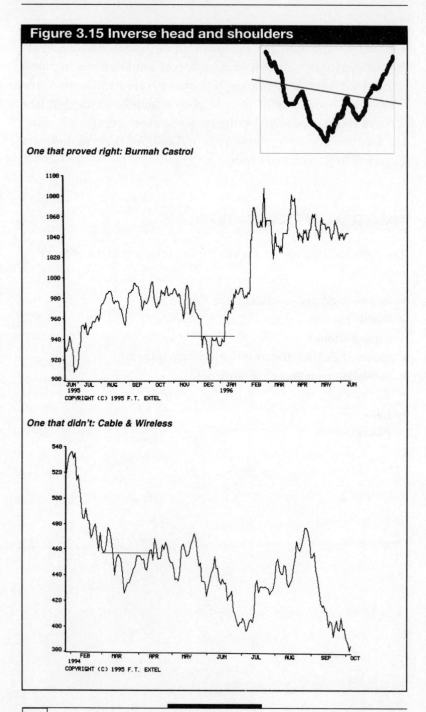

One that proved right: Burmah Castrol

COPYRIGHT (C) 1995 F.T. EXTEL

One that didn't: Cable & Wireless

COPYRIGHT (C) 1995 F.T. EXTEL

Figure 3.16 Ascending triangle

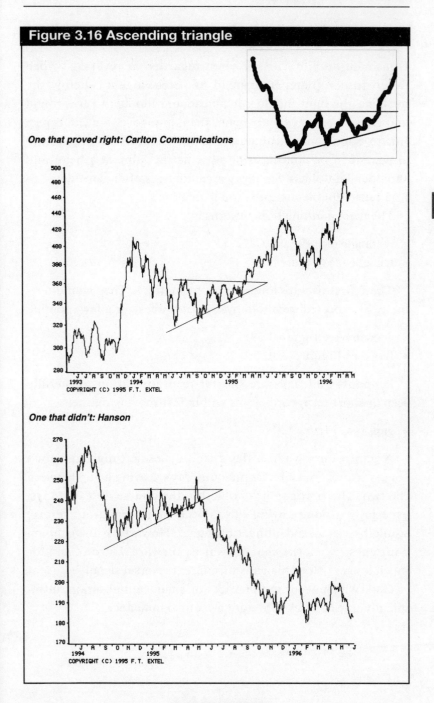

One that proved right: Carlton Communications

COPYRIGHT (C) 1995 F.T. EXTEL

One that didn't: Hanson

COPYRIGHT (C) 1995 F.T. EXTEL

CONTINUATION PATTERNS

Continuation patterns are often regarded as reversals which failed to complete. If, instead of 'breaking out' below the neckline, the right shoulder in a head and shoulders turns round and goes determinedly up again, then, in theory, you can expect this to point to a continuation of the trend which might have appeared to be coming to a close as the 'almost a head and shoulders' unfolded. Similarly a rectangle is often considered to be a failed double- or triple-top formation.

The main continuation patterns are:

- **rectangle** (see Figure 3.17);
- **triangle** (see Figure 3.18).

These first two are longer-term formations. They would normally be expected to unfold over several weeks or a few months.

- **pennant** (see Figure 3.19);
- **flag** (see Figure 3.20).

Pennants and flags are shorter-term formations, generally seen as short-term corrections within fast-moving markets.

- **gaps** (see Figure 3.21).

A gap occurs when a day's trading range (high and low) occurs entirely outside the previous day's, leaving a gap between the two. The first gap or two within the course of a few days, especially accompanying one of the four formations above, would be seen as a continuation signal. However, if the gapping continues – then the chartist warns, 'Beware! It won't last for much longer.' Now, the gaps turn into a reversal signal.

Gaps which occur in the prices of small capitalisation, infrequently traded stocks, do not have any significance.

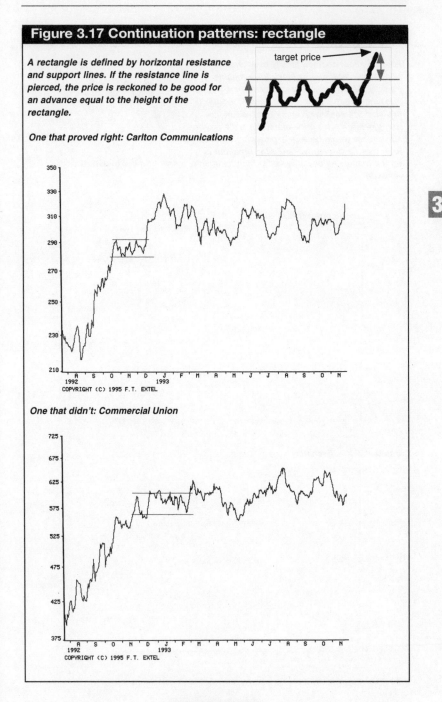

Figure 3.17 Continuation patterns: rectangle

A rectangle is defined by horizontal resistance and support lines. If the resistance line is pierced, the price is reckoned to be good for an advance equal to the height of the rectangle.

One that proved right: Carlton Communications

One that didn't: Commercial Union

Figure 3.18 Continuation patterns: triangle

Four points of contact, ideally over about 4 – 10 weeks, are reckoned to make for a reliable triangle. As with the descending triangle (Figure 3.11) the target after breakout (which should see high volume) is given by the base of the triangle. If the price goes to and fro right into the apex, there would be less expectation that the prior trend will resume. And if the breakout is on the triangle's downside rather than its upside, it may turn out to denote a reversal.

One that proved right: British Biotech

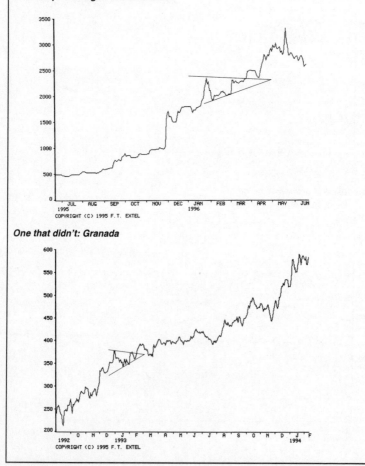

One that didn't: Granada

Figure 3.19 Continuation patterns: pennant

A 'pennant' is a small triangle, formed over a week or two at most, after a significant and rapid change in price. The price target following a pennant is measured in a very different way from that for its larger cousin, with the 'measure' being the price difference travelled by the preceding 'significant and rapid change in price'. This amount is projected from the breakout to arrive at the target.

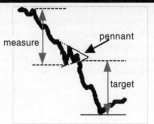

One that proved right: M L Laboratories

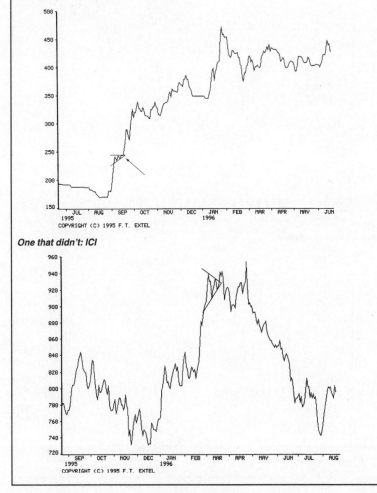

One that didn't: ICI

Figure 3.20 Continuation patterns: flag

A 'flag' has the same context and meaning as a pennant and also forms in a short time span of days or weeks, not months. However, its defining lines are parallel rather than converging. The price target after a flag is calculated in the same way as for a pennant.

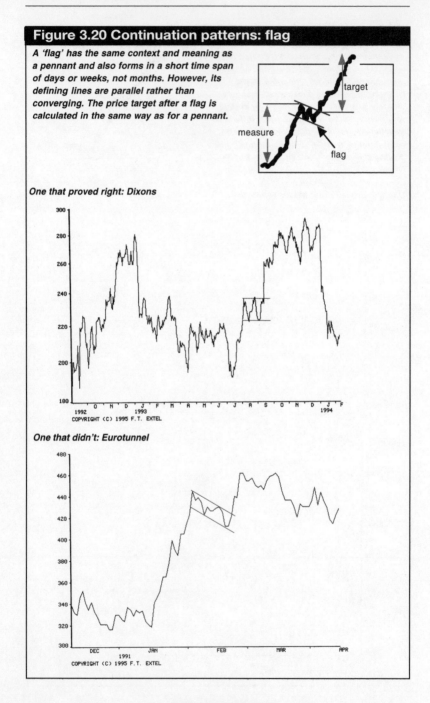

One that proved right: Dixons

One that didn't: Eurotunnel

Figure 3.21 Continuation patterns: gaps

A gap – only detectable in a bar chart – occurs when the whole of a day's trading takes place outside the previous day's range. One or two gaps are considered to portend continued movement in the direction of the gap, but a third or fourth may signal its end. Here, the breakout from the prior trading range saw a 'breakout gap', followed three days later by a continuation or 'runaway gap'. But the next signifies too much of a good thing: it turns out to be an 'exhaustion gap', showing that the preceding rapid trend has run its course. Subsequently, the exhaustion gap (and probably the continuation gap too) are 'filled'.

One that proved right: Cordiant

One that didn't: Devro

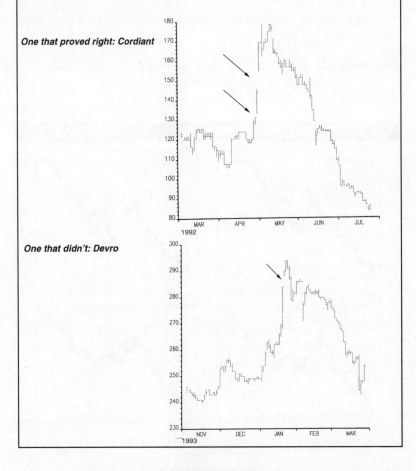

The technical analyst will interpret continuation patterns in the wider context. For instance, what is the long-term trend within which the triangle or pennant occurs? Is there a trend to be continued? Do the rectangle and its breakout form above the resistance line of an uptrend (that would be promising), or below its support line (treat with caution).

One sub-species which needs mention is the 'wedge'. All chartists talk of wedges, but the term has different meanings to different chartists. To some, 'wedge' is a synonym for 'triangle'. To others, a wedge is a different continuation pattern altogether. A third crowd sees the wedge as not a continuation pattern at all, but one of reversal.

Irrespective of nomenclature, triangles come in various forms, (see Figure 3.22) including:

- **symmetrical**: pointing horizontally towards the right-hand side of the chart;

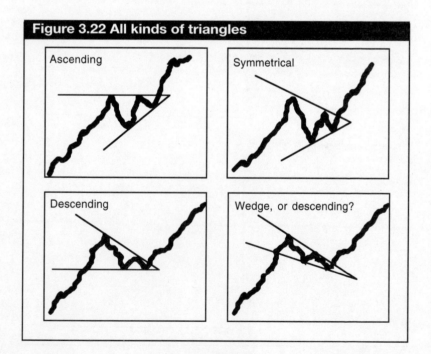

Figure 3.22 All kinds of triangles

- **ascending**:   horizontal resistance, rising support;
- **descending**:   horizontal support, falling resistance.

Some chartists see each triangle shape as possessing its own special signal. In particular, descending triangles are often seen to lead onto weakness, especially when they occur in bear trends, and vice versa. Others consider shape to be of less interest than whether the breakout occurs on its top or bottom side.

3

'The contents are always the same: it's how you shake them, and where you put the mirrors that makes for variety. And just as with a kaleidoscope, after a while you realise you could go on forever.'

THE SUPPORTING CAST 4

Secondary signals to support the main conclusion

- Volume and relative strength
- The professional's chart
- Momentum
- Other mathematical indicators

With highs, lows, corrections and trends being so damnably difficult to spot, chartists make use of a large supporting cast of secondary signals. These, it is hoped, will support conclusions drawn from the pattern of prices by pointing to the same conclusion from different evidence. Sometimes, it's the same evidence, treated in a different way.

VOLUME

Volume is the amount of business done. If 10m shares in ICI are traded today and only 1m tomorrow, that could say something. If 50m were traded the week before last and only 4m last week, that could say even more. Chartists follow volume by incorporating a second set of bars below the primary share price graph, as in Figure 4.1.

Volume has been considered an important indicator ever since the days of Dow, who said, 'Volume goes with the trend,' and he meant the main trend or correction, not minor reactions. In other words, if the share or market is in an upward trend, then volume should be relatively high on the days the market rises, and light when it is reacting or pausing; likewise, when the trend is heading down, the market should see high volume on down days. Accordingly, a significant 'breakout', that is a major price move occurring within a short period such as a few days, should be supported by heavy volume. If it is not, say the chartists, it's wise to be suspicious about whether it will last.

This fits with the adage: 'Bull markets start in light volume.' The very first inklings of a bull market are minor reactions in a long term downtrend. For months, successive movements downwards have been accompanied by heavy volume and minor bouts of optimism by light volume. What's different this time? Nothing you'd notice.

It's when the volume turns up along with an upwards breakout in price that you know, in theory at any rate, that the reversal has finally arrived. But it began, invisibly, with low volume.

RELATIVE STRENGTH or 'SHARE PRICE RELATIVE'

Relative strength is a measure of how a share (or group of shares) is faring compared to the rest of the market. ICI may be down 5 per cent this month, but if the other FT-SE 100 stocks are on average down 10 per cent, ICI is doing well.

Relative strength should be a familiar concept to anyone with any experience of stockmarket investing. Independent analyses of unit trust performance, for instance, are based on comparisons with the rest of the sector, not their absolute gains or losses. Suppose your small companies unit trust is down by 20 per cent. You might find some solace in knowing that on average, other small companies trusts were down by 40 per cent. You'd find none in the knowledge that they were ahead by 10 per cent.

Relative strength is calculated by choosing an index against which to compare your investment, and creating a ratio between the two. Figure 4.1 gives an example.

Figure 4.1 Relative strength

	1 March	1 June	change
Share price	254p	298p	+17.3%
All-Share Index	1700	1750	+ 2.9%
Indexed share price*	0.149 or 14.9	0.170, or 17.0	+14.1%

* Or 'Relative Strength': share price divided by the All-Share (or another) Index. Normally, the result would be multiplied by 100 so that the result isn't a fraction.

Looking at a share's relative strength will tell you how much of its price movement is due to the strength of the company and how much is due to market-wide sentiment. If you like the look of a share because its share price has recently begun to strengthen, it would be as well to check that it is indeed the share that's doing well, and not simply the market as a whole. Blue-chip shares with rising relative strength are the leaders in a bull market: these are the shares that should move ahead fastest on the next leg of the uptrend. Chapter 9 gives several examples of diverging price and relative strength, including the chart for BTR.

The relative strength figure depends arbitrarily upon when it was first calculated and whether the share price is heavy (e.g. 950p) or light (42p), so no significance should be placed on whether it is 6 or 66. What is important is what happens to it subsequently. Is it rising or falling? Can you detect a trend?

Relative strength is habitually shown as a third plot on the chart. Shown below is a typical chartist's concatenation of share price, volume (in millions of shares) and relative strength in a single presentation. It takes a bit of studying to decide which scale links to which line and crossovers, as here where the relative strength line encounters the share price bars, are inevitable from time to time (and are of no significance). The share in

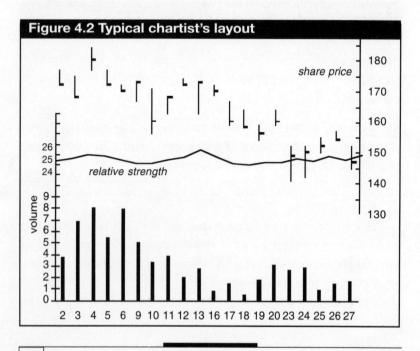

Figure 4.2 Typical chartist's layout

question has been weak since the middle of the month, but it is apparent that the market has too, for the share's relative strength is steady (see Figure 4.2).

A minority of chartists apply trend lines to the relative strength line with much the same enthusiasm as they employ the technique on share prices. If a 'top' forms in the relative strength line, it could confirm or portend the same pattern in the price itself.

BREADTH AND THE ADVANCE/DECLINE LINE

4

Breadth is a measure of how many shares are rising compared with how many are falling and staying unchanged in price. This might sound like the job the FT-SE 100 or All Share Indices do, but breadth is different and gives a genuine second opinion.

The Indices are weighted according to the market value of the companies they include. The FT-SE Index will react more to a 2 per cent change in price by Glaxo, which is worth around £30bn, than it will to a 2 per cent change in price by Tomkins, a £3bn minnow. The All-Share Index is calculated in the same way.

Breadth, however, gives each company just one vote: if Glaxo's up, there's a 1 in the advance column. If Tomkins is down, a 1 goes in the decline column. And a company worth just £2m gets a vote too: breadth includes all the tiny companies that don't even make it into the All-Share. On the London Stock Exchange, that's about 2,900 companies (whereas the 'All-Share' just includes about 800).

The *Financial Times* reports the three figures – 'rises, falls and same' – in its daily market statistics, on the page before the London share prices. Most of the time, these figures marry up well with what's happening to the main indices: a preponderance of risers when the index is moving ahead, and vice versa. From time to time, however, there are some curious divergences. The chartist view is that it's healthy for a rally in the indices to be confirmed by breadth.

The advance decline line combines the two main components of breadth into a single figure, by calculating the difference between the number of risers and the number of fallers. The advance decline line is subjected to the same trend analysis as any other line a chartist lays his hands on.

Breadth is primarily of concern to investors interested in the market as a whole, especially those who trade in FT-SE options.

MOMENTUM

Just like a pendulum, a share price which is moving up or down has to stop, at least momentarily, before it can move in the opposite direction. Some would take this parallel further: before its momentary stop between changes of direction, it is noted, the pendulum *slows down*. Ha! The slowing down *is an indicator* of an impending stop! And therefore of a *change of direction*! Technical analysts feel that share prices too are inclined to slow down before they stop and change direction. Therefore they measure how fast a price is changing, as well as the change itself.

Momentum measures the change in the share price since five, ten or 20 days ago (or any other period – as with moving averages, you have to find a figure that suits you, or the share you are analysing). The result can be negative or positive – in other words, it oscillates around zero. This secondary indicator is therefore known as a momentum oscillator and the table in Figure 4.3 demonstrates how it is calculated. Figures 4.4 and 4.5 depict the results when the figures are transformed into a graph.

A typical method of choosing which periodicity (i.e, whether five days, ten days, etc) to use would be to calculate from historic figures a periodicity that would have generated reliable signals. The choice is crucial, as shown by Figure 4.5 which adds a ten-day oscillator to the graphs already presented in Figure 4.4.

Figure 4.3 Calculating an oscillator

trading day	price	5-day oscillator	10-day oscillator
0	40		
1	42		
2	44		
3	46		
4	48		
5	50	10	
6	52	10	
7	54	10	
8	56	10	
9	58	10	
10	60	10	20
11	62	10	20
12	63	9	19
13	63	7	17
14	63	5*	15
15	63	3	13
16	63	1	11
17	61	–2	7
18	59	–4	3
19	57	–6	–1
20	55	–8	–5

* For instance, this figure is the difference between the price on day 14 – 63p – and that five trading days earlier on day 9 – 58p.

The terms 'over-bought' and 'over-sold' are often used in conjunction with oscillators. A share whose oscillator has moved into the top of its normal range could be called 'over-bought,' and vice versa. An alternative rendition is that a peak or 'V' by itself, wherever it is in the range, indicates these conditions. And, emphasising the oscillator's secondary status, the view is sometimes taken that it is neither peaks and 'Vs', nor extremities, that make signals, but rather occasions when the oscillator fails to replicate the basic patterns of the share price graph.

The momentum oscillator idea brings out one of the differences in philosophy between pure fundamentalists and chartists. Any share making a significant transition in value does so on a 'two steps forward, one backward' path. The fundamentalist

Figure 4.4 Momentum oscillators

A momentum oscillator measures the difference between today's share price and the price five (or ten, or 20 . . . you choose) days ago, based on the theory that share prices, like moving bodies, slow down before they change direction... usually.

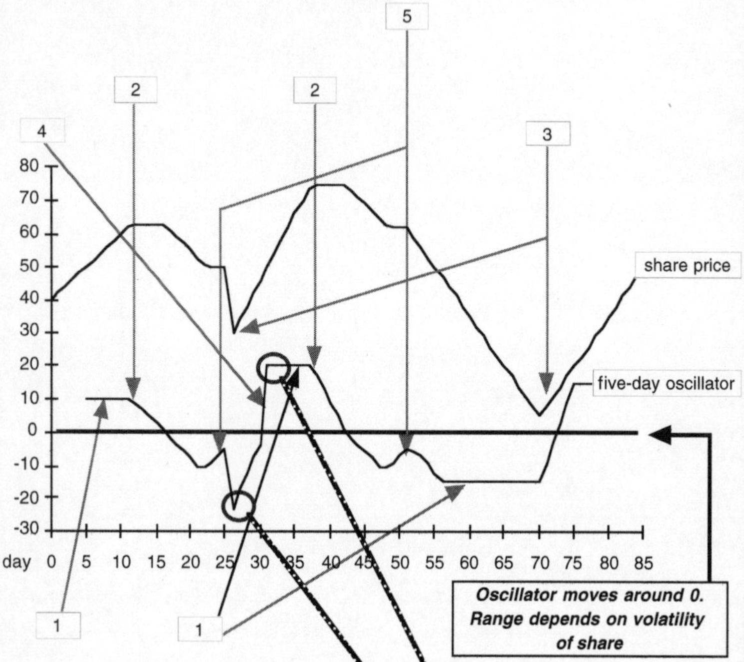

share price

five-day oscillator

Oscillator moves around 0. Range depends on volatility of share

Oscillators are secondary indicators intended to confirm primary signals. A typical rule might be . . . sell the share only when its oscillator changes direction within the outermost positive extremity of its range – here, say 18 or more, and buy on a change of direction within the outermost negative extremity – here say –20

'Sell' signal, *assuming primary indicators also favour 'sell' (signal is false)*

'Buy' signal, *assuming primary indicators also favour 'buy' (signal is successful)*

Key to Figure 4.4 Momentum oscillators

1   Oscillator steady whilst share price is changing because change is same amount each day (i.e. it is not getting any faster or slower).

2   Oscillator gives warning of impending price fall because the price steadies before it falls. See the text. Compare with note 3.

3   Oscillator gives no warning of impending price rise because there is no pause between the fall and rise.

4   Five-day oscillator bounds back when six-day-ago price fall leaves calculation.

5   Share price fall pauses, so oscillator rises, anticipating possible reversal of short-term trend. See the text.

4

Figure 4.5 The effect of periodicity

To formulate a secondary indicator from changes in the share price, you need to decide its periodicity, or how many days' worth of changes to use, e.g. last three days, last 25 days. To illustrate the effects of changing this input, the two graphs below show the different signals generated by a five-day oscillator and a ten-day oscillator. Note that in practice, you would not rely solely upon the oscillator's signals and you might use a different rule to identify signals from that used here (which is 'change of direction within the extremity').

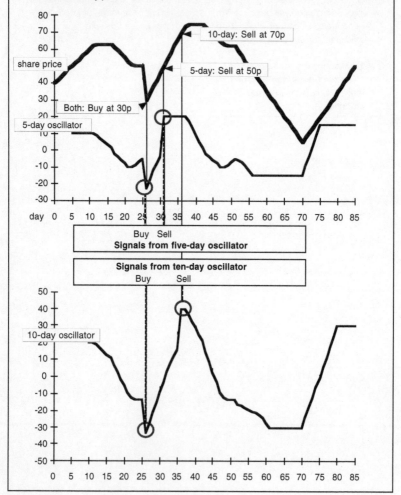

isn't interested in the fact that a share headed up from 100p to 200p will pause at 160p or fall back to 140p. A pure chartist, unattuned to the brighter fundamental prospects for the same share, would likely find his oscillator in or close to 'over-bought' territory all the way up to 200p, and would in any case be unlikely to receive an over-sold, or 'buy' signal. However, the same animal works well for heavily cyclical shares.

WELLES WILDER'S RSI

J Welles Wilder Jr stands high in the chartists' Hall of Fame. He plugged technical analysis into the newly invented spreadsheet and came up with some enduring concepts, of which the most famous is RSI, or the Relative Strength Index. This was launched (along with ADX and DMI, but we don't tackle those here) in his 1978 book, *New Concepts in Technical Trading Systems*, which memorably compared the search for 'directional movement' to chasing the end of a rainbow.

Despite the similarity in name, Welles Wilder's RSI is absolutely nothing to do with 'relative strength' discussed on pages 87–89. RSI is a sophisticated oscillator, measuring the current strength of the share price against its own recent history. Relative strength (often known as 'the share price relative') measures the strength of the share price against the strength of other comparable shares. The UK charting firm, Investment Research of Cambridge, which uses both indicators, calls Welles Wilder's RSI, 'rate of change' (or ROC) to distinguish it from relative strength.

RSI compares recent rises with recent falls and works out which tendency (rises or falls) is dominating, and by how much. It's simpler than it sounds, but nevertheless ingenious. The formulation is set out in the table in Figure 4.6 and Figure 4.7 shows how it looks on a chart.

In this example, the averages of rises and falls are calculated over the previous ten days. Welles Wilder in fact recommended

Figure 4.6 Calculating Welles Wilder's RSI

trading day	price	rise	fall	10-day average of rises	10-day average of falls	Relative Strength ratio of average rises to average falls	Relative Strength Index 100 − (100/[1+ relative strength])
0	140						
1	142	2					
2	140		2				
3	139		1				
4	137		2				
5	139	2					
6	141	2					
7	143	2					
8	142		1				
9	144	2					
10	146	2		1.2	0.6	2	66.7
11	148	2		1.2	0.6	2	66.7
12	149	1		1.3	0.4	3.3	76.5
13	149			1.3	0.3	4.3	81.3
14	150	1		1.4	0.1	14	93.3
15	150			1.2	0.1	12	92.3
16	150			1	0.1	10	90.9
17	148		2	0.8	0.3	2.7	72.7
18	146		2	0.8	0.4	2	66.7
19	144		2	0.6	0.6	1	50

using 14-day averages, but as always, this is a 'what works best?' situation. Many modern adherents of RSI use shorter periods, sometimes as little as five days.

Unlike the momentum oscillator, RSI always fits into a pre-determined range, of 0 to 100. This is achieved by the indexing adjustment, which is what happens in the last column in Figure 4.6. This means its extremities (the levels above and below which it is 'over-sold' or 'over-bought') can be predetermined too, whereas with the oscillator, you have to identify what the range in order to judge where the extremities lie. It is pretty much an iron rule that over-bought and over-sold, when using

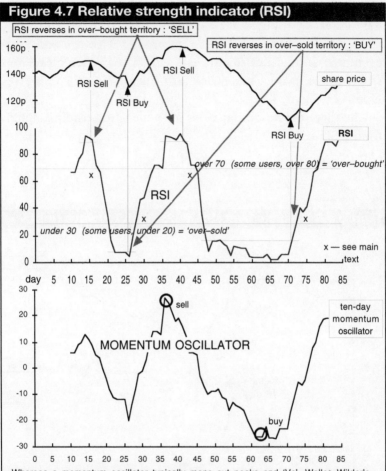

Figure 4.7 Relative strength indicator (RSI)

Whereas a momentum oscillator typically maps out peaks and 'Vs', Welles Wilder's Relative Strength Index turns the same share price history into plateaux and wider valleys: it spends more time out of 'neutral territory'.

There are several ways to identify trading signals from RSI. Here, the rule used for some eerily successful trading signals is a reversal of RSI (its going back past a recent level) within over-bought or over-sold territory. In this case, RSI gives more signals, and more accurately, than does the oscillator.

Note that, like a momentum oscillator, RSI is generally used as a secondary indicator, with the chartist looking to it to confirm some other feature in the data, such as a double bottom in the share price or significant divergences between the share price and RSI patterns, before acting on its signals.

Welles Wilder's RSI, are set at 70 and 30 respectively, which are the figures he proposed. Occasionally chartists use 80 and 20.

A great strength of RSI, as compared with a momentum oscillator, is that it does not react with a jerk when a previous step-change in the share price falls out of the reckoning (see Note 4 in Figure 4.4).

The three most popular rules for generating trading signals from RSI are:

• reversals within over-extended territory;

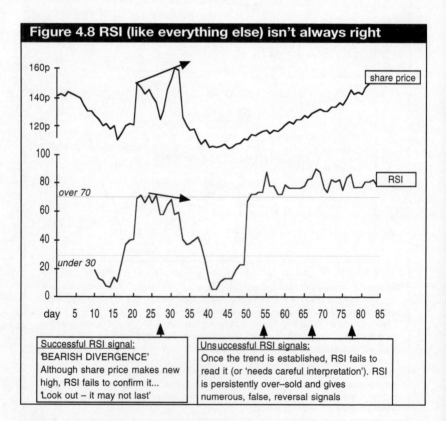

Figure 4.8 RSI (like everything else) isn't always right

Successful RSI signal:
'BEARISH DIVERGENCE'
Although share price makes new high, RSI fails to confirm it...
'Look out – it may not last'

Unsuccessful RSI signals:
Once the trend is established, RSI fails to read it (or 'needs careful interpretation'). RSI is persistently over–sold and gives numerous, false, reversal signals

- RSI crossing from over-extended to neutral territory. This rule would have generated trades at the points marked 'x' in Figure 4.7;
- divergences or 'failure swings' (Figure 4.7).

Just as with other indicators, RSI does not work well if a long-running up or down trend is in place. This can be seen in Figure 4.8. Welles Wilder himself suggested that it was best used in sideways trending (or 'trendless') markets.

STOCHASTIC

4

Stochastic is the most complicated of the modest selection of secondary indicators discussed here. It was devised in the 1960s and the main claimant to its authorship is Dr George Lane, a fellow-countryman of J Welles Wilder Jr.

The theory behind 'stochastic' is that as an upward trend begins to tire, closing prices will fall towards the bottom of the recent range of intra-day prices, whereas they will have been towards the top of that range when the trend was in full flow. In downtrends, closes are reckoned to be towards the bottom of the recent range, this pattern likewise giving way as the downtrend fades. This is another variation on the concept of momentum – that share prices slow down before they turn round.

Stochastic therefore requires daily high, low and closing prices, and the formula relates today's close to the 'highest high' and 'lowest low' of the last so many days. A typical periodicity is ten days, with the ten-day result being 'smoothed' by taking its three-day average, known as 'Fast %D'. This three-day result is itself averaged, to produce 'Slow %D'. Both 'Ds' are indexed so as to stay within a range of 0–100. In the pre-spreadsheet 1960s, Dr Lane presumably had a mainframe at his disposal.

Trading signals are generated by crossovers by these two lines, Fast %D and Slow %D, and their own crossings of the usual 'over-sold' and 'over-bought' lines at 70 and 30 (or 80 and 20,

Figure 4.9 Calculating stochastic

1	2	3	4	5	6	7	8	9 %K*	10 Fast %D	11 Slow %D
trading day high	low	close	10-day high	10-day low	close minus 10-day low	high minus 10-day low	col. 7 divided by col. 8 times 100	3-day average of col. 9	3-day average of col. 10	
0	175	170	175							
1	177	168	176							
2	180	177	178							
3	182	172	180							
4	180	170	179							
5	180	167	179							
6	188	175	185							
7	188	177	186							
8	188	178	184							
9	185	177	184							
10	189	185	189	189	167	22	22	100		
11	193	186	193	193	167	26	26	100		
12	192	185	191	193	167	24	26	92.3	97.4	
13	199	188	197	199	167	30	32	93.8	95.4	
14	202	189	199	202	167	32	35	91.4	92.5	95.1
15	202	194	199	202	167	32	35	91.4	92.2	93.4
16	196	188	195	202	175	20	27	74.1	85.6	90.1
17	202	194	200	202	177	23	25	92	85.8	87.9

* As originally devised, stochastic used '%K' and 'Fast %D'. This formulation is too sensitive to 'noise' and is rarely used now. It is known as 'fast stochastic', and the version explained here, as 'slow stochastic'.

occasionally 85 and 15). Figure 4.9 shows the calculations for stochastic and Figure 4.10, the graphical result.

Figure 4.10 Stochastic

This technique uses recent intra-day highs and lows to generate two lines: 'Fast %D' and 'Slow %D'. Stochastic's followers look for a two-part signal to confirm a trade (again, this is usually a secondary indicator):

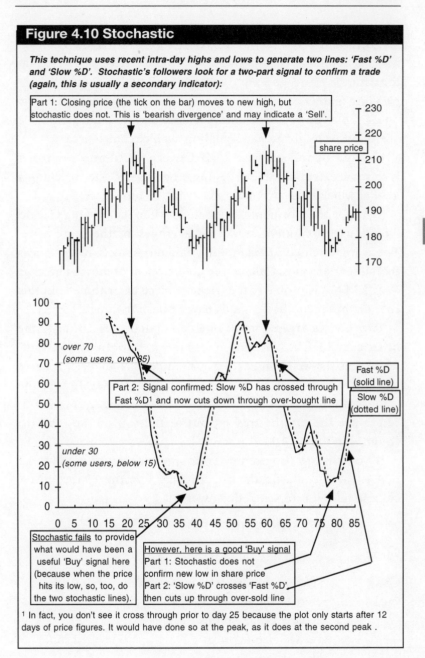

Part 1: Closing price (the tick on the bar) moves to new high, but stochastic does not. This is 'bearish divergence' and may indicate a 'Sell'.

share price

over 70
(some users, over 85)

Part 2: Signal confirmed: Slow %D has crossed through Fast %D[1] and now cuts down through over-bought line

Fast %D (solid line)

Slow %D (dotted line)

under 30
(some users, below 15)

Stochastic fails to provide what would have been a useful 'Buy' signal here (because when the price hits its low, so, too, do the two stochastic lines).

However, here is a good 'Buy' signal
Part 1: Stochastic does not confirm new low in share price
Part 2: 'Slow %D' crosses 'Fast %D', then cuts up through over-sold line

[1] In fact, you don't see it cross through prior to day 25 because the plot only starts after 12 days of price figures. It would have done so at the peak, as it does at the second peak .

MACD (MOVING AVERAGE CONVERGENCE-DIVERGENCE)

MACD combines the up-and-down characteristic of an oscillator with the ability to follow a trend, so in theory should help in trending market conditions – that is, when prices are persistently on the up or down. Momentum oscillators, RSI and stochastic are all prone to giving bad signals in such circumstances.

Unlike RSI and stochastic, MACD is not tied into a range: it is to some extent capable of 'going on going up' after reaching a level at which these two must steady off or turn down.

MACD, the brainchild of yet another American, Gerald Appel, uses 'exponential moving averages' of the share price. These are weighted calculations, giving more say to recent prices than to earlier ones. Calculating an exponential moving average – or 'EMA' – is probably the trickiest piece of arithmetic in this chapter, but then, the demands haven't been that high!

Two EMAs are required: one calculated over 26 days, the other over 13. The calculation requires a 'smoothing constant' which sets the weighting of the current day's share price relative to the reading from earlier days. For the 13-day figure, the smoothing constant is 2/13 = 0.15, and for 26 days, 2/26 = 0.075. These are the two figures set out at the top of the relevant columns in Figure 4.11.

If you wish to programme your spreadsheet to calculate an EMA, the formula in the cell for Day 1 in the 13-day EMA column (and it is repeated downwards) is:

$$=((1-(C\$3))*C4)+(C\$3*B5)$$

where:

C\$3	picks up the smoothing constant ...	0.15
C4	refers to the preceding calculation of the average (in this case the average of one price) ...	175
B5	takes in today's price ...	176

However, the readings can't be used for MACD until you have the first 26 days' prices fed into the calculation. (The EMAs in columns 4 and 6 are calculated in a parallel way – read on for the relevance of Column 6.)

Figure 4.11 Calculating MACD

				MACD	Signal line
1	2	3	4	5	6
trading day	price	13-day exponential moving average*	26-day exponential moving average*	13-day EMA minus 26-day EMA	10-day EMA of column 5
		0.15	0.075		0.2
0	175	175	175		
1	176	175.2	175.1	0.1	0
2	178	175.6	175.3	0.3	0.1
3	180	176.2	175.6	0.6	0.2
4	179	176.7	175.9	0.8	0.3
5	179	177	176.1	0.9	0.4
6	185	178.2	176.8	1.4	0.6
7	186	179.4	177.5	1.9	0.9

* see text

If you're less technically minded, refer back to Chapter 2 in which long- and short-run moving averages were used to generate crossovers and trading signals (remember the 'golden cross'?). This is simply a souped-up version of the same thing.

Neither of the moving averages are plotted on the chart: what is plotted is the MACD line, which is simply the difference between these two: that's what happens in column 5 in the table. Finally the MACD line is itself subjected to an exponential moving average adjustment (column 6), in just the same way as George Lane arrived at 'Slow %D' for stochastic. The smoothing adjustment used for this is normally 0.2, for a ten-day moving average. This line is known as 'the signal line' (sometimes Slow %D is given the same title). Its function is to be crossed by MACD: when this happens, there's your indicator.

Figure 4.12 MACD copes with persistent trends

The first step in MACD is to create 13- and 26-day moving averages (in fact, these are 'exponential' moving averages – see text) of the share price. These two series are not themselves graphed. However, the difference between them is: this is the MACD line on the lower graph. MACD is then itself averaged, to generate a second line (the 'signal line'). Subject to confirmation from other indicators, MACD indicates a 'sell' when it crosses down through the signal line, and a buy when it moves back up through it.

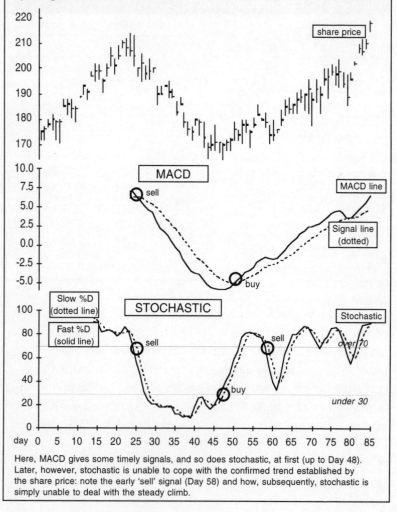

Here, MACD gives some timely signals, and so does stochastic, at first (up to Day 48). Later, however, stochastic is unable to cope with the confirmed trend established by the share price: note the early 'sell' signal (Day 58) and how, subsequently, stochastic is simply unable to deal with the steady climb.

For some reason, the MACD formula receives far less tweaking by its practitioners than those of other secondary indicators. This happens, of course, but there's a remarkable measure of agreement that the exponential moving averages are calculated over 26 and 13 days, and that the signal line comes from a ten-day EMA.

MACD's ability to cope with persistent trends is very evident in Figure 4.12. It's worth noting that RSI would have encountered similar problems to stochastic had it met up with that

THERE ARE MANY MORE...

4

(unusual) bull run in the share price.

By no means has this been a complete guide to secondary signals. It does, however cover most of the indicators in regular use in the UK, and also gives you a flavour of how secondary signals are constructed. Is that the right word? Perhaps one should say 'shaken' as the process strikes me as similar to playing with a kaleidoscope. The contents are always the same: it's how you shake them, and where you put the mirrors that makes for variety. And just as with a kaleidoscope, after a while, you realise you could go on forever. But you're not going to see much you haven't seen already.

US enthusiasts, often abetted by having studied physics to PhD level, turn out an engulfing stream of indicators. If you read the books in the bibliography, you will encounter MESA (Maximum Entropy Spectral Analysis, the True Strength Index, SD–TSI (Slope Divergence TSI Filter), and 'Up Move and Then a Pullback – Adam's Entry Technique.' Happy reading.

For a comprehensive (but still incomplete) discussion of secondary indicators which does not require monstrous mathematical expertise, try *Schwager on Futures: Technical Analysis*. Although set in the world of US futures and options markets, its coverage would not be lost on a keen UK stockmarket chartist.

'Along with the elegance of candlesticks comes a raft of theory and an attractive new terminology. Who could resist discovering the meaning of a "bearish engulfing formation" or a "morning star"?'

HOW THEY DO IT IN JAPAN

And increasingly here too – an introduction to candlestick charting

- Steve Nison reveals all
- Candlestick construction
- Candlepower
- Candlesticks tested

Candlesticks are a Japanese method of depicting open, high, low and close prices in a more elegant and readable way than the Western method of adding ticks to either side of a bar. They can be thought of as squint-free (or perhaps, low-squint) versions of their Western counterparts.

Although devised in the late 19th century, candlestick charting was virtually unknown outside Japan until Mr Steve Nison, an employee of Daiwa Securities in New York, wrote *Japanese Candlestick Charting Techniques* in 1991. As charting books go, this has been a best-seller and a sequel duly arrived in 1994: *Beyond Candlesticks*. For stockmarket followers, the second book is preferable as it includes all the basics, but focuses on shares whereas the first concentrates on the futures markets.

Along with the elegance of candlesticks comes a raft of theory and an attractive new terminology. Who could resist discovering the meaning of a *'bearish engulfing formation'*, or a *'morning star'*? A cult subject took off. Suppliers of charting software rushed to include a candlestick option in their packages. Mr Nison is surely counting the advance on his third book even now, as less well-known charting hacks labour to add candlesticks to their own coverage.

Candlestick charting techniques echo the general Japanese fascination with the diminutive by emphasising the significance of very short-term movements in share prices. Western techniques are also alive to these, as for instance with the 'key reversal' and 'spike' discussed in Chapter 3. But the candlestick tool kit includes many more variations on this theme. Candlestick techniques are also considered to place more emphasis on reversal signals and less on continuation ones, than Western methods.

BODIES AND SHADOWS

The basic approach and terminology of candlesticks are explained in Figure 5.1. As you can see, candlesticks are functionally identical to the open-high-low-close bars with ticks.

However, instead of using ticks, a black or white 'fat bar' is superimposed on a thin one. If black, the closing price was lower than the opening price. If white, the reverse applies. Candlestick charts are much easier to read than bars with ticks.

The most obviously significant type of candlestick is that with a long body, either black or white. These denote major one-

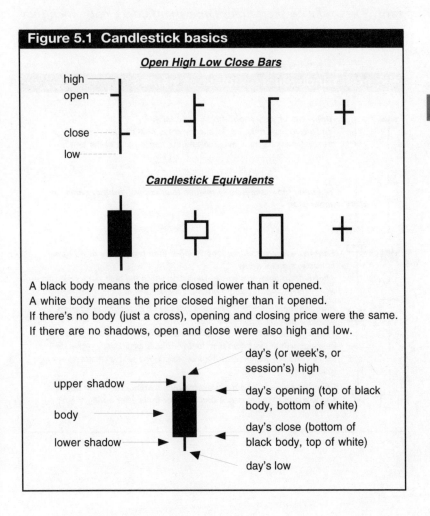

Figure 5.1 Candlestick basics

Open High Low Close Bars

high
open
close
low

Candlestick Equivalents

A black body means the price closed lower than it opened.
A white body means the price closed higher than it opened.
If there's no body (just a cross), opening and closing price were the same.
If there are no shadows, open and close were also high and low.

upper shadow → day's (or week's, or session's) high
day's opening (top of black body, bottom of white)
body → day's close (bottom of black body, top of white)
lower shadow → day's low

day price moves. These are considered to set up significant support or resistance levels for the future, except when they break such earlier support or resistance levels, thereby signifying that all bets are off.

Several other individual candlestick types are given their own names, of which the main ones described in Figure 5.2. These can occur at any time and they are not always seen to be important. *They take on their names and significance only when they occur in specific circumstances, such as after a rally or decline.*

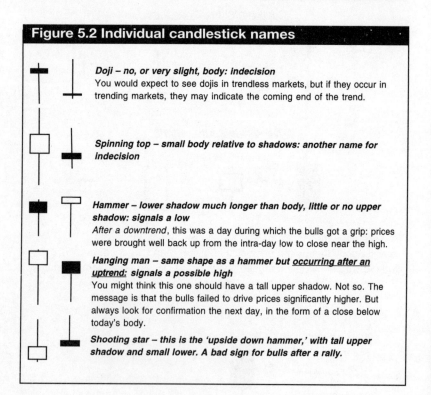

Figure 5.2 Individual candlestick names

Doji – no, or very slight, body: indecision
You would expect to see dojis in trendless markets, but if they occur in trending markets, they may indicate the coming end of the trend.

Spinning top – small body relative to shadows: another name for indecision

Hammer – lower shadow much longer than body, little or no upper shadow: signals a low
After a downtrend, this was a day during which the bulls got a grip: prices were brought well back up from the intra-day low to close near the high.

Hanging man – same shape as a hammer but <u>occurring after an uptrend:</u> signals a possible high
You might think this one should have a tall upper shadow. Not so. The message is that the bulls failed to drive prices significantly higher. But always look for confirmation the next day, in the form of a close below today's body.

Shooting star – this is the 'upside down hammer,' with tall upper shadow and small lower. A bad sign for bulls after a rally.

CANDLESTICK PATTERNS

The most commonly recognised candlestick patterns are described in Figure 5.3.

Figure 5.3 Candlestick patterns

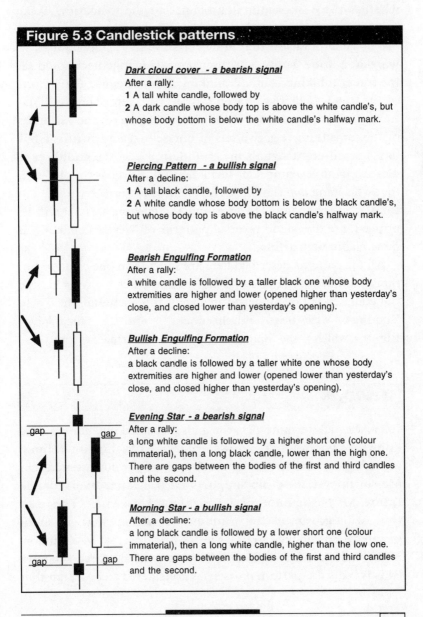

Dark cloud cover - a bearish signal
After a rally:
1 A tall white candle, followed by
2 A dark candle whose body top is above the white candle's, but whose body bottom is below the white candle's halfway mark.

Piercing Pattern - a bullish signal
After a decline:
1 A tall black candle, followed by
2 A white candle whose body bottom is below the black candle's, but whose body top is above the black candle's halfway mark.

Bearish Engulfing Formation
After a rally:
a white candle is followed by a taller black one whose body extremities are higher and lower (opened higher than yesterday's close, and closed lower than yesterday's opening).

Bullish Engulfing Formation
After a decline:
a black candle is followed by a taller white one whose body extremities are higher and lower (opened lower than yesterday's close, and closed higher than yesterday's opening).

Evening Star - a bearish signal
After a rally:
a long white candle is followed by a higher short one (colour immaterial), then a long black candle, lower than the high one. There are gaps between the bodies of the first and third candles and the second.

Morning Star - a bullish signal
After a decline:
a long black candle is followed by a lower short one (colour immaterial), then a long white candle, higher than the low one. There are gaps between the bodies of the first and third candles and the second.

5

This is but a cursory treatment of the subject. In his books, Mr Nison devotes pages of earnest discussion, for instance, to interpretation of 'dark cloud cover' if the second day's close is just above the halfway mark of the previous day's body, and to whether there is greater significance to the formation if the second day's opening is above the first day's high.

The general idea is that one bearish sign is rarely enough to warrant a trade, but two or three appearing together should set the trader thinking. And all thinking is done against the context of the trend. If there's no trend to reverse ... etc. The combination which prompts a buy or sell action can be several instances of the same thing (e.g. two sets of dark cloud cover within a few days) or different signals in combination (e.g. the middle candlestick in an 'evening star' formation taking the form of a *doji*, for an 'evening *doji* star'). Not all of these patterns are unique to candlestick charting. The morning and evening stars, it will be noticed, are the island reversal patterns of Western charting, if more elaborately defined.

All the patterns described here are short-term ones, but do not think that the technique stops short. Candlestick charting has the full complement of longer-term signals too, including the Three Buddhas — the head and shoulders — and the Three River Bottom, which is the Japanese equivalent of a triple bottom.

WINDOWS

In candlestick terminology, the gaps discussed in Chapter 3 are known as windows. Windows are termed 'rising' or 'falling' according to whether they occur in uptrends or downtrends, and are considered to set up support and resistance levels for the future. Mr Nison quotes a Japanese market saying: 'The reaction will go until the window,' meaning that a small countertrend will tend to finish at the price level set by a window in the main trend. Just as with Western analysis, three windows (this is judged a pattern in itself) is considered to be a sign that the trend which opened them is ready to turn round.

Whereas exhaustion gaps are subsequently 'filled' when the price returns to the level at which the gap occurred, windows are described as being 'closed'.

JACK SCHWAGER'S TESTS

In *Schwager on Futures: Technical Analysis*, the author rounds up a chapter on candlestick charting (a chapter guest-written by Mr Nison), with an account of some tests he ran on the technique. Noting that candlestick signals tend to be much more compact than Western ones, in that many of them take place over one to three days, he suggests they may lend themselves to less subjective interpretation than the classic Western patterns. He therefore programmed a computer to look for and trade upon ten candlestick signals, including the *doji*, the engulfing patterns and the hammer. The testing was carried out on five years of back prices from ten futures markets such as sugar and Eurodollars.

The results were described as unencouraging. In fact they were disastrous. For instance, by trading on the basis of a single hanging man or hammer, losses were recorded in seven of the ten markets tested, with an overall loss of $17,000 of the opening capital of $60,000 exposed.

This was a very simplistic, in fact unfair, test. If candlestick charting provided a free lunch, Mr Nison would have eaten it, instead of writing about the technique. It should however serve as a warning to the uninitiated.

The charts in Chapter 9 use candlesticks, and provide some commentary on how this technique has worked in the context of the UK's top shares in the months prior to writing. These charts throw up many examples of the individual candlesticks and patterns described here, often marking highs and lows, though less reliably at *significant* highs and lows (highs terminating, or lows preceding, *clearly worthwhile price moves*).

> *'Most investors have come
> across point and figure charts
> but few understand them.'*

IS THE PRICE MOVING? REALLY MOVING?

Point and figure charts

6

- The basic idea
- How to do it
- Trends, signals and price targets

Point and figure charting is in many ways the antithesis of candlestick charting. For the candlestick chartist every little ripple of the share price could have a message. How wide was the range on the day? How did today's closing relate to yesterday's? And the candlestick chartist has a predominantly short-term view. How much money might we make today? Tomorrow? Two weeks can be a long time to the candlestick chartist. Point and figure chartists aren't interested in short-term fluctuations. If the price moves less than a predetermined amount – typically 1 per cent – they don't even record it. And point and figure chartists are inclined to look for long-term gains. They can hail as a success a price prediction that takes years to come true. Other chartists do this too, but it's more typical of the point and figure technique.

Most investors have come across point and figure charts but few understand them. The reason is that point and figure charts do not have a 'sensible' horizontal scale.

Everyone has come across a conventional chart that they have difficulty understanding – it takes a bit of effort, for instance, to figure out what a stochastics chart is trying to convey. But at least the problem is in the line itself, not the scales.

With point and figure charts, even the scales are against you. These charts defy a first, uninformed, inspection. The first sideways inch on a point and figure chart could signify a month; the next, a year. This is so counter-intuitive, that many people call it a day after 30 seconds.

Point and figure charting, which was devised in the US in the last century when speculators used it to record prices from 'the tape' in share-pushing bucket shops, is a heroic effort to sort the wheat from the chaff. The chaff is the 'market noise' – minor day-to-day ripples in the share price which are neither here nor there in the view of point and figure chartists. They distill 'price action' into two essential questions:

1 Is the price *moving*?
and that means, 'Is it moving *seriously*?' – it's not enough for a 150p share to move by a penny. The point and figure chartist

wants to see it move by, say 2p, or 3p. If the price today doesn't move by the point and figure chartist's selected quantum, he simply ignores it – *today's modest share price movement does not get entered on his chart unless and until it becomes part of his quantum.*

2 Is it going up or down?

HOW TO COMPILE A POINT AND FIGURE CHART

To translate this concept into a charting method, two questions must be answered:

1 What constitutes a move forward? If the price is established in a trend, either up or down, how big a move represents real progress? For a 150p share, this could be, say 2p. For 40p share, it would probably be 1p.

2 What constitutes a change of direction? This is normally a bigger amount than the answer to Question 1. The 150p share which has advanced from 120p and now moves on to 152p would seem to be continuing its trend. But what if it moved to 148p? Is that a change of trend? The point and figure chartist says it isn't. Not by itself: moving back 4p could easily be chaff. He wants to see it move back more seriously, say to 144p.

Let's assume we're dealing with a 150p share, and have settled on 2p as the 'move-forward measure.' The chartist calls this 'the box'. And we'll adopt 6p as the 'change of trend measure'. This is 'the reversal'. To the chartist, this is a 'three-box reversal' method – the most widely used system.

The table in Figure 6.1 gives share prices for MistryNuShops, which floated on the Stock Exchange on 1 August at 140p. Against each day's price are high and low 'reference points', which you could also think of as opposing sets of goal posts. These are the levels to which the share price has to move to register either a continuation of the trend or its reversal. When the price hits a reference point, an entry is made on the chart and the reference points are revised. If the share price is moving upwards, the reference points are 2p above the last reference point reached and 6p below it. If the share price reverses so far as to hit its low reference point, the goal posts are moved. Now the direction is downwards, so the new low reference point is 2p below the last reference point registered by the share price. The new high reference point is 6p above the same figure. The reference points are always 8p apart. Further explanation would be less useful to you than simply working through the table.

Figure 6.1 Compiling a point and figure chart for MistryNuShops

Box size: 2p. Reversal: 3 boxes

price	today's reference points		comments	entry on chart	revised reference points for tomorrow	
	high	low			high	low
Aug 1 140						
2 142	142	134	up 2: start with an X	X at 142 as price has moved up one box	144	136
3 140	144	136	down 2: needs to go down 6	nothing		
4 139	144	136	still above low ref			
5 137	144	136				
8 139	144	136				
9 141	144	136				
10 143	144	136				
11 142	144	136				
12 144	144	136	hits high ref	add an X above existing X	146	138
15 148	146	138	hits high ref	and again	148	140
16 148	148	140	hits high ref	and again	150	142
17 149	150	142				
18 149	150	142				
19 150	150	142	hits high ref	and again	152	144
22 150	152	144				
23 150	152	144				
24 148	152	144				
25 146	152	144				
26 144	152	144	hits low ref	move over a column, down a row*, fill with 0s to 144	150	142
29 142	150	142	hits low ref	add a 0 below existing 0s.	148	140
30 140	148	140	hits low ref	and again	146	138
31 138	146	138	hits low ref	and again	144	136

Sep 1	137	144	136				
2	138	144	136				
5	138	144	136				
6	130	144	136	goes through low ref:	add 0s down to 130	136	128
7	134	136	128				
8	138	136	128	goes through high ref:	move over a column, up a row*, fill with Xs to 138	140	132
9	142	140	132	goes through high ref:	add Xs to 142	144	136
12	141	144	136				
13	143	144	136				
14	147	144	136	goes through high ref:	add Xs to 146	148	140
15	151	148	140	goes through high ref:	add Xs to 150	152	144
16	152	152	144				
19	151	152	144				
20	157	152	144	goes through high ref:	add Xs to 156	158	150
21	159	158	150	and so on.		160	152

* this is the convention

6

Figure 6.2 MistryNuShops share prices

Aug		Sep		Oct		Nov	
1	140	1	137	1	156	1	111
2	142	2	138	2	154	2	108
3	140	5	138	3	152	5	105
4	139	6	130	4	150	6	108
5	137	7	134	5	151	7	111
8	139	8	138	8	151	8	114
9	141	9	142	9	151	9	113
10	143	12	141	10	148	12	112
11	142	13	143	11	145	13	115
12	144	14	147	12	142	14	118
15	146	15	151	15	143	15	121
16	148	16	152	16	140	16	124
17	149	19	151	17	137	19	123.5
18	149	20	157	18	134	20	127
19	150	21	159	19	131	21	130
22	150	22	160	22	128	22	129.5
23	150	23	160	23	125	23	132.5
24	148	26	160	24	122	26	135.5
25	146	27	159	25	119		
26	144	28	159	26	119.5		
29	142	29	157	29	116.5		
30	140	30	158	30	113.5		
31	138			31	110		

There's a complete set of prices for MistryNuShops running to late November in Figure 6.2 and Figure 6.3 provides a complete chart. This includes a few annotations to explain its compilation. To give subsequent readers of the chart some idea of timing, it is customary when making the first entry of the month, to substitute the initial letter of the month for the X or O. Sometimes, these are placed above and below the columns, instead. Figure 6.4 is a conventional chart for the same share prices.

Figure 6.3 Point and figure chart for MistryNuShops

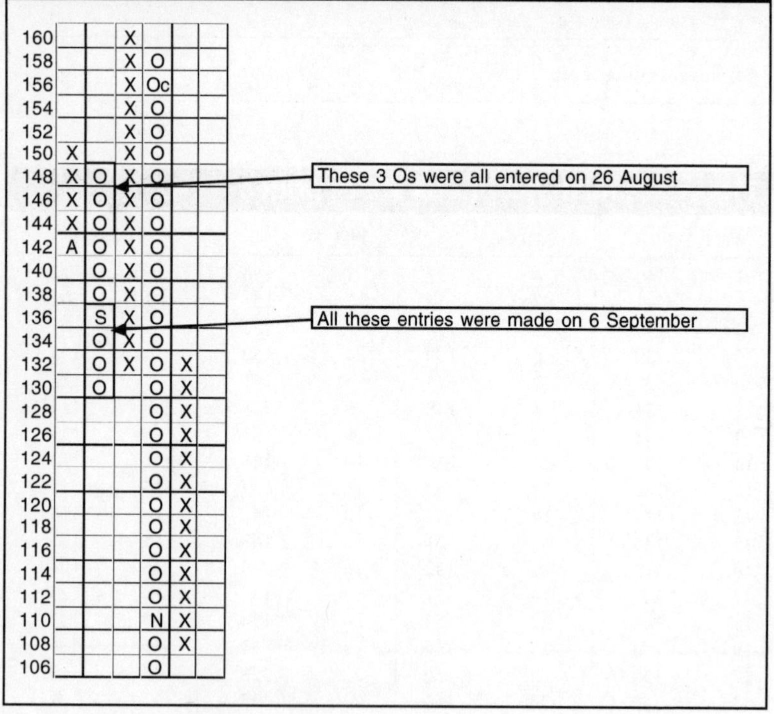

Price						
160			X			
158			X	O		
156			X	Oc		
154			X	O		
152			X	O		
150	X		X	O		
148	X	O	X	O		
146	X	O	X	O		
144	X	O	X	O		
142	A	O	X	O		
140		O	X	O		
138		O	X	O		
136		S	X	O		
134		O	X	O		
132		O	X	O	X	
130		O		O	X	
128				O	X	
126				O	X	
124				O	X	
122				O	X	
120				O	X	
118				O	X	
116				O	X	
114				O	X	
112				O	X	
110				N	X	
108				O	X	
106				O		

These 3 Os were all entered on 26 August

All these entries were made on 6 September

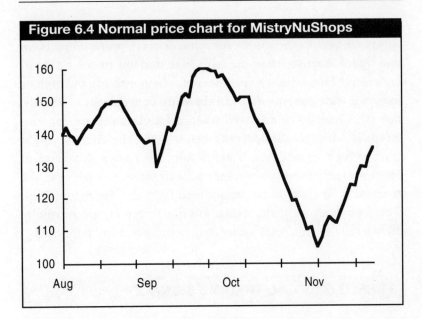

Figure 6.4 Normal price chart for MistryNuShops

The effect of the point and figure method is to compress the five main trends in the conventional chart into five simple columns of Os and Xs. The wrinkles within the broad trends have disappeared, even that not-so-minor one at the start. The highs and lows all translate into point and figure (but not with total accuracy: some of them are likely to be just short of one box 'out'). In fact, highs and lows: that's all you're looking at; it would even be possible to take out the Os and Xs. They're left in for tradition's sake, but when you think about it, this differentiation adds nothing. All you need is an arrow on the end of the last column to show you which way the price is moving currently. In fact, on the Japanese version of these charts, known as *kagi*, a single line snakes up and down the page.

Assuming you are now comfortable with how point and figure charts are compiled, there are three other points you should know. First: you don't have to use a reversal amount which is larger than the box. Some currency traders, looking at minute-by-minute movements in prices, move to a new column on every change of direction. As their graphs are updated by computer, paper size is not a restraint. Second, professional point and figure chartists often use daily high and low prices, not closing prices. This raises the problem of whether to use the high or low on a wide-ranging day, but there are conventions ... Finally, box sizes have to be adjusted when price extremes are encountered. If MistryNuShops sank below 100p, the chartist might start using a 1p box, and if below 20p, a 0.5p box. Likewise, at 500p, a switch to 5p boxes might be warranted. In each case, the reversal factor would be maintained (e.g. at 1.5p, below 20p). These changes of scale, which are not frequent, are normally allowed to flow into each other as if nothing else had happened.

TREND LINES AND TRADING SIGNALS

Trend lines can be drawn on point and figure charts just as they are on conventional charts, and they are breached in just the same way too. Also, the classic formations – head and shoulders and so on can be plainly observed. Figure 6.5 gives examples of trend lines and trading signals in point and figure format. However, some practitioners recommend that trend lines should always be drawn at fixed, pre-determined angles: respectively at 45 degrees for lines progressing upwards, such as support and resistance in an uptrend, and at 135 degrees for lines progressing downwards. This approach is summarised in Figure 6.6.

US point and figure specialist, Thomas Dorsey (see **Further Reading** on page 237) advocates using the point and figure method to track all conceivable series and is a champion of the NYSE Bullish Percent Index which was devised in the 1950s by Chartcraft, a venerable US chart publisher. This is a measure of the proportion of NYSE stocks showing new point and figure 'buy' signals (those stocks running X columns which have newly risen above the previous X column). This measure is itself tracked on a point and figure chart.

Figure 6.5 Point and figure trades

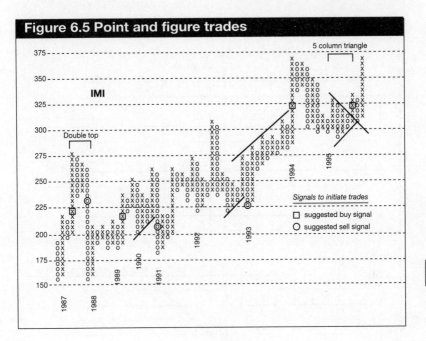

Figure 6.6 Fixed angle trend lines

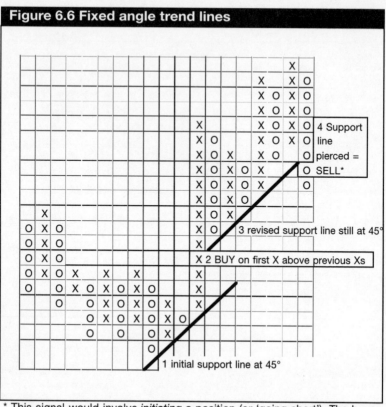

* This signal would involve *initiating* a position (or 'going short'). The buyer at point 2 would probably have taken at least some profits already.

'THE COUNT'

Point and figure chartists use an unusual method of targeting future price movements, known as 'the count'. The basic idea is that in a bottom or a top, each reversal on the chart represents an argument that will come to be settled later by an almighty bust-up. Twenty arguments are deemed likely to fuel a bigger bust-up than ten. The reversals are simply counted from the number of columns which the bottom or top took up. See Figure 6.7. Another technique counts the boxes vertically to derive a price target. This is equally adventurous.

Figure 6.7 Point and figure horizontal count

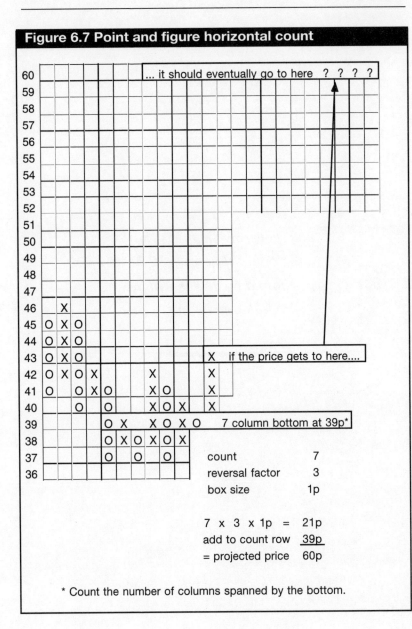

* Count the number of columns spanned by the bottom.

'The recurring theme is that of the cycle: that ups will be followed by downs will be followed by ups.'

A QUICK GUIDE TO THE CHARTIST GOSPELS

- Rabbit explosion in Pisa
- Elliot waved them on
- Prechter waved goodbye
- Gann's strange ideas
- Coppock fades in the 80s

Some colourful names and even more colourful theories are regularly quoted by technical analysts. The recent past has usually been foretold by someone now in their grave. The trouble is, it's always someone different. In fact, few modern practitioners subscribe rigidly to any of the theories outlined here.

The recurring theme is that of the cycle: that ups will be followed by downs will be followed by ups. Just like the tide, the moon and the seasons. You are correct, say these great theorists, in commenting that these natural cycles are more susceptible to forecasting than the stockmarket, but maybe not so much more.

FIBONACCI

Leonardo Fibonacci lived in Pisa around the time its Tower was built. A mathematician, he is credited with promoting the decimal numbering system. He didn't get his name on that one, but succeeded with 'Fibonacci Numbers', a series which you probably covered briefly at school before forgetting it. In fact, Fibonacci was not the original discoverer of the numbers. They had earlier been recognised by the Greeks and Egyptians – the design of the pyramids is said to demonstrate familiarity with this series of numbers.

Fibonacci stumbled across his numbers when trying to project how a rabbit population would grow from a single pair. After assuming (amongst other things) that all levels of descendants would be born in pairs he arrived at the magic Fibonacci series set out in the last column of Figure 7.1. It doesn't stop at 144: it goes on forever. Apart from being a lip-smacking version of compound interest, it has several interesting properties:

- each number after the first is the total of the previous two (so 34 for Month 9 equals 13 from Month 7 plus 21 from Month 8, etc);
- the ratio of each number (after the first few) to the next one is 0.618, or – the same thing – of each number to its predecessor, 1.618;

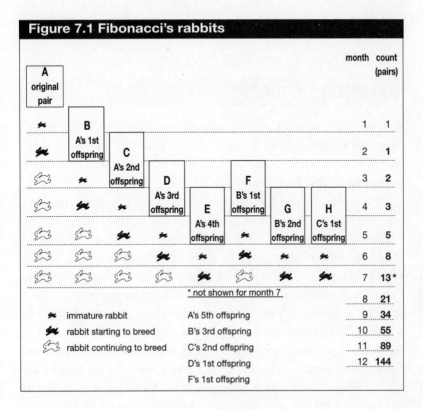

Figure 7.1 Fibonacci's rabbits

								month	count (pairs)
A original pair									
🐰	**B** A's 1st offspring							1	1
🐰	A's 1st offspring	**C** A's 2nd offspring						2	1
🐇	🐰	A's 2nd offspring	**D** A's 3rd offspring		**F** B's 1st offspring			3	2
🐇	🐰	🐰	A's 3rd offspring	**E** A's 4th offspring	B's 1st offspring	**G** B's 2nd offspring	**H** C's 1st offspring	4	3
🐇	🐇	🐰	🐰	A's 4th offspring	🐰	B's 2nd offspring	C's 1st offspring	5	5
🐇	🐇	🐇	🐰	🐰	🐰	🐰	🐰	6	8
🐇	🐇	🐇	🐇	🐰	🐇	🐰	🐰	7	13*

* not shown for month 7

	month	count
	8	21
🐰 immature rabbit A's 5th offspring	9	34
🐰 rabbit starting to breed B's 3rd offspring	10	55
🐇 rabbit continuing to breed C's 2nd offspring	11	89
D's 1st offspring	12	144
F's 1st offspring		

- the ratios for alternate numbers (after the first few) are 0.382 and 2.618.

There is no record of Fibonacci having put his Numbers to use for investment purposes. However, he did notice that his series cropped up outside rabbit demographics (where it doesn't apply at all, if you sweep away Fibonacci's assumptions). Many of nature's finest creations are apparently designed along the lines of Fibonacci Numbers, including spiral galaxies, musical tones and the Venus de Milo's vital statistics. Some people therefore consider them imbued with cosmic significance. One such was Ralph Elliott.

ELLIOTT WAVE THEORY

Ralph Elliott was an American accountant who, during an illness in the late 1920s, set to work to examine many decades worth of stock price charts. He did so in exacting detail: down to half-hour price movements.

Elliott decided he had spotted several regular patterns from his work, and that these patterns were knitted together by Fibonacci Numbers. This potent concoction, which he termed 'Nature's Math') surfaced in 1934. At the time, Wall Street, which had in 1933 shown the first serious recovery from the Crash, was experiencing a downturn, feared by some to herald a return to misery. Elliott informed investors that the downturn was a mild bull market 'corrective wave', due to turn round at any time and make way for the next 'cardinal wave'. Cardinal waves head in the direction of the trend, and the trend was up. As to where the market was going in 1934, he was right. It recovered a 20 per cent downturn by the year end and went on to double within 30 months.

Mystified but impressed stockbrokers learned that these two waves belonged to a pattern of eight, and the eight were a cycle which had been driving the stockmarket for a century or more. The basic idea of Elliott Wave Theory is shown in Figure 7.2.

Where did Fibonacci come into it? In three ways. First, the basic pattern of 5 + 3 = 8 uses Fibonacci Numbers. As does the 21 up, 13 down – and a total of 34 – make-up of the next degree. Next, the vertical extent of waves related to Fibonacci's Numbers, with the ratios 1.618 and 0.618 and others explaining how far each advance or retracement extends. Finally, time spans between turning points were often Fibonacci numbers. In his book, *Nature's Law: The Secret of the Universe* published in

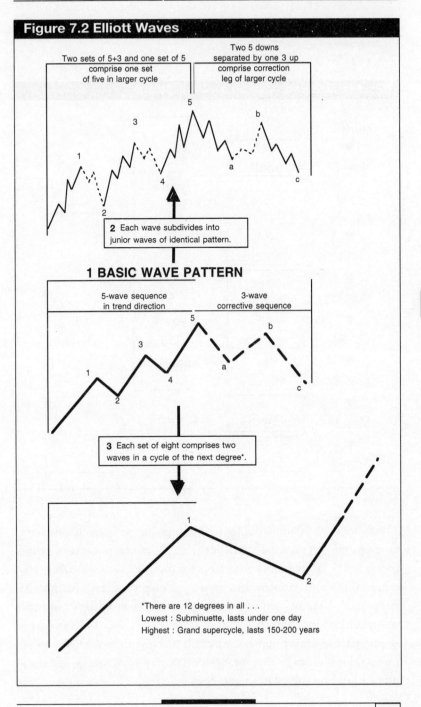

Figure 7.2 Elliott Waves

Two sets of 5+3 and one set of 5 comprise one set of five in larger cycle

Two 5 downs separated by one 3 up comprise correction leg of larger cycle

2 Each wave subdivides into junior waves of identical pattern.

1 BASIC WAVE PATTERN

5-wave sequence in trend direction

3-wave corrective sequence

3 Each set of eight comprises two waves in a cycle of the next degree*.

*There are 12 degrees in all . . .
Lowest : Subminuette, lasts under one day
Highest : Grand supercycle, lasts 150-200 years

7

1945, Elliott cited the list of significant highs and lows in the Dow Indexes shown in Figure 7.3.

Figure 7.3 Elliott Waves on Wall Street

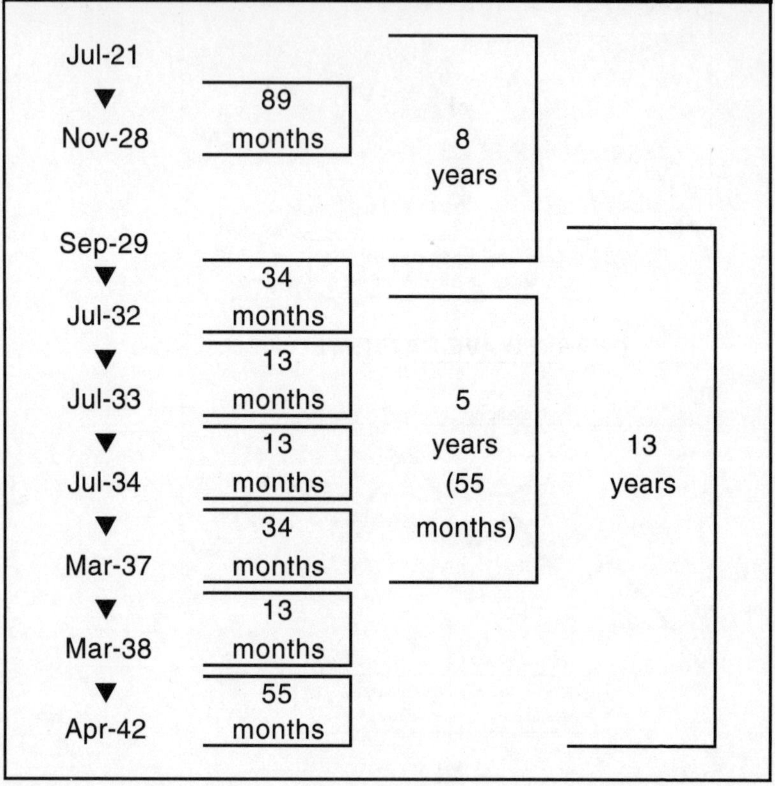

Jul-21			
▼	89		
Nov-28	months	8 years	
Sep-29			
▼	34		
Jul-32	months		
▼	13		
Jul-33	months	5 years	13 years
▼	13	(55 months)	
Jul-34	months		
▼	34		
Mar-37	months		
▼	13		
Mar-38	months		
▼	55		
Apr-42	months		

All the time spans (that he had somewhat selectively chosen), he pointed out, were constituents of Fibonacci's series, some twice over! He was not troubled by the fact that Nature's law counted in both months and years, whichever suited. Rather, he suggested, the law worked through crowd psychology, and the crowd did count in both. In an upwave, he argued, bulls progressively get the upper hand, eventually taking an asset price to an unsustainable peak. The inevitable fall in prices forces out optimists and puts the bears in charge.

Despite this encouragement from then-current events, Elliott did not suggest his analysis enabled precise forecasting. Sometimes the pattern missed a sequence or extended one. In fact, he formulated a Rule of Alternation: if the market failed to match the wave sequence once, it would shortly do so again. However, he was pretty sure that the third wave (running between Points 2 and 3 in Figure 7.2), if you could spot it, was almost always the best. It lasted the longest and moved the furthest. If you could spot it. The problem, he acknowledged, was that since smaller waves exist within larger ones, 11 times over, wave identification was an art, not a science.

After Elliott's death in 1948, his works fell into relative obscurity, a passage assisted by a long-lasting bull market on Wall Street. There was barely a need to call the turning points. But in the 1960s, cognoscenti revived interest in Elliott Wave Theory by picking out more Fibonacci Numbers. A low in 1970 was correctly forecast on the basis that preceding lows had occurred 21, 13, eight, and five years previously. And had there not been a low 55 years before that of 1962? There had.

Enter Robert Prechter, Yale graduate, ex-rock drummer and technical analyst at Merrill Lynch. Prechter relaunched Elliott by co-writing an interpretation of Nature's Law, in 1978. All the Dow's trends to date, it turned out, could be accurately assigned to Wave Theory, with a corrective fourth wave which had started in 1965 about to complete and an upwards-heading 'impulse' wave (the re-christened cardinal) due to follow. This would end, he forecast, in the late 1980s, to complete the upwards phase of one of Elliott's 'supercycles' (one degree beneath the grand supercycle), which had kicked off in 1932.

Prechter left Merrill Lynch to launch an investment newsletter and manage money on his own account, and throughout the early 1980s, called the market with great accuracy. In 1984, he beat all records by scoring a four-month gain of 440 per cent in his managed fund. Prechter appeared to have turned Elliott's art into his own science. Until 1987. Prechter foresaw a correction in the October but expected it to be modest. He had targeted his impulse wave to terminate at 3,686 in 1988. When October 1987 turned out to be a less than modest reversal, he assigned it 'end of Wave 5' status. Long-term investors, who had been advised – when the Dow stood at 2,600 – to hang on through the October correction, were now advised to get out at 2,000. And to be ready to get back in again, in the early 1990s at around 400 (which would neatly have returned the Dow to its 1929 peak).

Such is life. The Dow sped back to its 1987 peak, and with one pause for breath, carried on upwards. Around the time, Prechter suggested it should be 400, it was heading to 4,000. Prechter still writes his newsletter, but it no longer attracts the coverage it received in the 1980s.

Prechter wasn't the only Elliott Wave Theorist. In the futures and options markets, 'Elliotticians' spot his waves on timespans measured in all units of time from minutes upwards, and in instruments from orange juice futures to interest rates. He would surely have been surprised, as he insisted his waves only occurred in generalised fields such as stockmarket indices.

The stockmarket too continues to attract Elliott-inspired analysis, also applied to individual stocks as well as the indices. Elliott has probably achieved a modest immortality. His five-up, three-down patterns crop up remorselessly, though rarely predictably (as he warned) and the issue of whether this is a great third wave, and from where a 62 or 38 per cent correction should be measured, are such entertaining topics that they may well last market commentators for all time.

GANN

Unlike Elliott, his contemporary WD Gann was a keen market trader. Not a successful one, it is said, but that hasn't prevented his books *How to Make Profits Trading in Commodities* and *Truth of the Stock Tape* from gaining a following. What Gann did share with Elliott was a belief that the universe kept faith with Fibonacci, when it wasn't keeping faith with Gann.

Perhaps his most popular bequest to the charting community was the proposition that there is generally a round figure relationship between price and time. For instance two units of price (say 2p) for every unit of time (say per day) or lp to 2 days, or 3 to 2 or 1 to 1 (it's best to cover as many eventualities as you can get away with) and so on. These formulae were turned into 'fanlines' which supposedly give guidance as to where support and resistance will be encountered. See Figure 7.4.

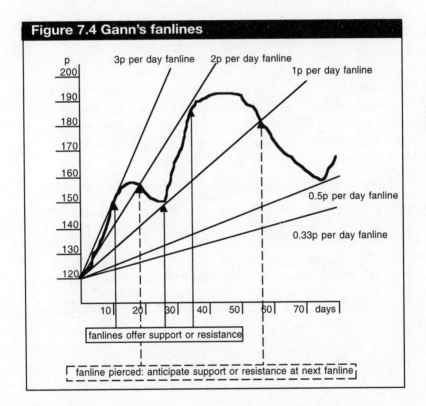

Figure 7.4 Gann's fanlines

7

Fanlines are meant to be drawn from significant lows or highs, especially all-time lows and highs. And in profusion: Figure 7.4 is restrained in using only five fanlines: a charting programme worth its salt will slot in nine or more with a click of the mouse.

Gann also came up with the cardinal square, an alternative means of predicting which prices would prove significant in future by offering support or resistance (the square does not tell you which). This is set out in Figure 7.5.

Figure 7.5 Gann's cardinal square

prices on the centre column and centre row will offer primary support/resistance in future

156	157	158	159	160	→	and so on	→	→	→		
155	114	115	116	117	118	119	120	121	122	123	124
154	113	80	81	82	83	84	85	86	87	88	125
153	112	79	54	55	56	57	58	59	60	89	126
152	111	78	53	36	37	38	39	40	61	90	127
151	110	77	52	35	26	27	28	41	62	91	128
150	109	76	51	34	25	24 all time low	29	42	63	92	129
149	108	75	50	33	32	31	30	43	64	93	130
148	107	74	49	48	47	46	45	44	65	94	131
147	106	73	72	71	70	69	68	67	66	95	132
146	105	104	103	102	101	100	99	98	97	96	133
145	144	143	142	141	140	139	138	137	136	135	134

prices on the diagonals will offer secondary support/resistance in future

There's more to Gann than these two concepts, but the rest is in a similar vein. Together with his ideas on significant anniversaries (such as one year) and multiple-of-an-eighth retracements and advances, he had virtually every point on the chart tabbed. Like Elliott, Gann achieved a comeback from the grave during the 1980s, but does not attract the same level of serious discussion.

COPPOCK

I am grateful to Robert Ansted of the *Investors Chronicle,* an expert on Coppock, for much of the following.

'Crowds do too much too soon,' said Edwin SC Coppock in a 1962 essay, 'The Madness of Crowds.' This described some research he had been doing on behalf of his Texas investment advisory firm, Trendex Research Group. He went on ...'They overdo. When they get an urge to speculate, their concerted demand forces prices up at a rate far greater then the growth of the company into which they are buying. Likewise. when they liquidate holdings or make short sales during a panicky decline, they ignore basic economic facts. They overdo because they are motivated by emotion rather than reason.' This all sounds right on the mark to anybody who has experienced one or two stock-market cycles.

Coppock wanted to turn these observations into 'a practical technique to aid long-term investors who wish to minimise risk.' Believing that a key driver in crowd psychology was how recently it had experienced a serious hit on its wallet, he turned to his local church and asked its officials how long the average person needs to grieve following a bereavement or other traumatic event. Eleven to 14 months, was the answer.

Coppock then formulated a memorable indicator. On a rolling basis, he calculated percentages for how much the Dow Jones Average had moved over the previous 14- and 11-month periods. These two figures were added together and turned into a ten-month weighted moving average. The result was a momentum oscillator (see Figure 4.3) to which he attached a simple rule: *Buy when it moves up whilst below zero.* 'The curve has been highly satisfactory as a profit maker,' said Coppock. A modest claim for a Texan.

Coppock was neither the first nor the last to formulate a momentum oscillator, but his inspiration of setting its periodicity according to how long bereavement depresses the emotions produced impressive results. The curve had identified the beginning or near-beginning of all four major surges in the Dow Index from 1948 to 1962. He arrived at a formula which picks up major lows but is not so sensitive that it called for action on what turned out to have been a minor reactions to the prevailing trend.

And when do you sell? You don't, at least not in the original Coppock scheme of things. He was an advisor to US institutional investors, who always had strong cashflows coming in from the public. His purpose was to help them time the investment of those cashflows by avoiding tops and amassing cash until the crowd was bent on another speculative surge. He didn't envisage that they would ever need to sell 'the market'. He did however note that the curve had acted as a warning of major market tops.

In 1963. Harold Wincott, editor of the *Investors Chronicle* in the UK, came across Coppock' s work and applied it to the UK market, using figures going back to 1940. In those days without readily accessible computers, a short cut was made, of using a single rolling 12-month average rather than the 11- and 14-month figures which Coppock had devised. Wincott found the results of his analysis highly satisfactory and the *Investors Chronicle* has published its 'IC/Coppock Indicators' ever since. (They appear once a month in a table at the back of the magazine. Indices are provided for a dozen major stockmarkets.) Inevitably, Coppock's original trading rule was extended by treating a turndown when the index was above zero as a 'sell' signal. Further, a subsidiary 'buy' signal was identified – when the Coppock Index turns up whilst still above zero. The *Investors Chronicle* terms these signals 'unofficial'.

In the 1970s, the IC/Coppock indicator caught the UK market's highs and lows with great accuracy. The signals were rare – the whole decade saw just three 'buys' (all 'official') and four 'sells' – but most were gilt-edged. In particular, it called a perfect 'sell' and 'buy' at the top and bottom of the calamitous collapse from 1972 to 1975, which saw the index fall by over

70 per cent. However, since then the record has been mixed. It is set out in Figure 7.6.

The 1980s were queer territory for IC/Coppock. The indicator stayed above zero from 1977 to 1989, and therefore gave not a single official signal in that time. This demonstrates the severe

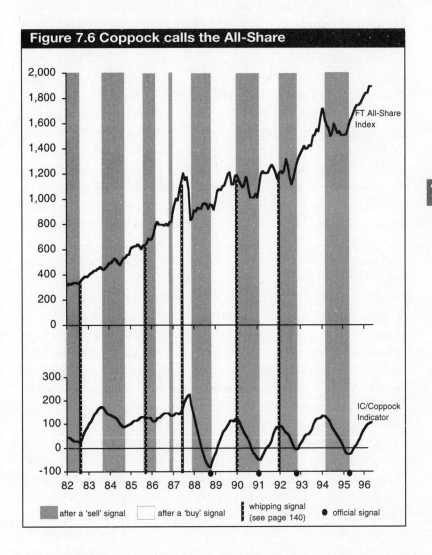

Figure 7.6 Coppock calls the All-Share

after a 'sell' signal   after a 'buy' signal   whipping signal (see page 140)   ● official signal

7

limitations of Coppocks original formulation. No investor could have afforded a signal which kept him out of the great 1980s' global bull market.

If the indicator was to be used at all then, the unofficial signals had to be considered. But these have had a poor record since 1983. First, and least, on several occasions these arrived in 'whipping sequences', with succeeding months delivering first one injunction then the opposite one – not at all what Coppock had in mind. More seriously, the 'sell' signals in 1983, 1985, 1986 and 1987 – after the October crash – were just plain wrong. The record in the 1990s has been rather better, or rather, less bad. Signals in the 1990s have been associated with market setbacks, but the timing has not been tight enough. Since October 1989, three IC/Coppock 'buy' signals (those of December 1989, January 1992 and November 1992) have arrived too late to put investors back into the market in time to put them ahead of where they would have been if they had simply ignored the 'sells' and held their portfolios. The ill effects of these signals have more than outweighed the benefits of the two 'good' 'sell' signals.

The problem is that the market often recovers, following a setback in very sharp spurts which either largely, or more than, make up for the preceding reaction. These are very evident in Figure 7.6 where strong gains may be seen in the month or two running up to each of the last three IC/Coppock 'buy' signals. In 1992, the market moved ahead by 15 per cent in just three months before the indicator gave a green light to buy. In the 1990s investors seem to need less grieving than 20 years ago. So why not shorten the formula? No doubt some have. But when will conditions swing around again?

In fact, the original Coppock 'buy signals only' approach should not be discarded. It is clear from Figure 7.6 that although the signals have tended to be late, they have on every occasion (and this even applies to the unofficial 'buy' signals except for that which occurred in 1986) been followed by a vigorous market for a minimum of four months before the next reaction began to take shape. The 'buy' signal could therefore be taken as marking conditions in which it would pay to take an aggressive approach to investing, for instance by gearing up a portfolio (i.e., buying shares with borrowed money) and buying call options, if that is the investor's style.

Figure 7.7 sets out in detail all the IC/Coppock signals since 1982 and compares the effects of following these (with 'sells' held to mean a switch into cash) with the strategy of simply buying the Index in 1982 and holding it through all ups and

Figure 7.7 Coppock compared with 'buy and hold' since 1982

'official signal'	date	signal	FT-A All-Share Index (FTAS)	FTAS change by next signal	Signal good or bad[1]	Slavish IC/Coppock [2] £	Buy and hold £
	7/82	buy	330	+2%	good	102	102
	8/82	sell	336	+6%	bad	102	108
	9/82	buy	357	+26%	good	128	136
	9/83	sell	449	+19%	bad	128	162
	10/84	buy	533	+19%	good	152	192
	9/85	sell	633	+8%	bad	152	208
	11/85	buy	684	−1%	bad	150	205
	12/85	sell	674	+17%	bad	150	239
	3/86	buy	787	+0%	−	150	239
	10/86	sell	788	+12%	bad	150	267
	1/87	buy	879	+12%	good	169	300
	4/87	sell	989	+8%	bad	169	326
	5/87	buy	1073	−23%	bad	131	251
	11/87	sell	828	+15%	bad	131	288
*	11/88	buy	949	+17%	good	153	337
	10/89	sell	1111	+6%	bad	153	357
	12/89	buy	1175	−2%	bad	149	348
	2/90	sell	1147	−4%	good	149	332
*	2/91	buy	1095	+6%	good	157	351
	12/91	sell	1156	+4%	bad	157	365
	1/92	buy	1203	+1%	good	159	370
	2/92	sell	1219	+5%	bad	159	390
*	11/92	buy	1284	+26%	good	201	492
	3/94	sell	1620	−3%	bad	201	475
*	4/95	buy	1566	+21%	good (so far)	243	574
	5/96		1890				

1 Based on performance between this signal and the next one
2 See text

downs. Even though no interest has been allocated to the Coppock strategy when it is holding cash, it is clear that 'buy' and 'hold' leaves IC/Coppock standing.

Coppock also devised a short-term indicator which is said to have worked well in the US, but not in the UK. He was working on a UK adaptation of this when he died in the mid-1980s.

OTHER CYCLISTS

Along with Dow, whose ideas were introduced in earlier chapters, Fibonacci, Elliott and Gann are the three biggest names in the charting pantheon. Coppock gets less attention than he deserves. Other residents include many proponents of the economic cycle: the idea that either investor psychology or economic lags, or both, predetermine, with one degree of accuracy or another, the ups and downs of the economy.

In the late 19th century Clement Juglar proposed a ten- to 12-year economic cycle. In 1923, a Professor Kitchin put his name on a 40-month stockmarket cycle. Both are still quoted to this day. Some claim that Kitchin had simply uncovered a system which the Rothschilds had been using secretly and profitably to forecast interest rates since the 1820s.

In Russia, Nikolai Kondratieff published in 1925 *The Long Waves in Economic Life*, an analysis of the history of capitalist economies since 1780. This postulated a 48-to 60-year cycle (neatly spanning Fibonacci's 55). As Stalin wanted to hear that capitalism was engaged in a process more terminal than a cycle, Kondratieff disappeared. However, another economist, Joseph Schumpeter, resurrected and revalidated the Kondratieff Cycle.

Keen technical analysts do not regard these cycles as mutually exclusive. In the manner of Elliott, they are inclined to see them as cycles of different degrees, and some make a pastime of superimposing the cycles upon each other to see when they all peak or bottom simultaneously. That would make a serious 'buy' or 'sell' signal. No-one has owned up to getting rich by using this technique.

'It would have been possible (although hard work) to identify ten straight charting success stories to cover in this chapter. More representatively, a streak of failure runs through it too.'

WHOEVER MADE MONEY FROM CHARTING?

8

- **Blowing off the roof**
- **Trader Vic beats Soros**
- **How Trout goes fishing**
- **Kroll cashes up**
- **Bolton's desert island request**

'It seems clear that under scientific scrutiny chart reading must share a pedestal with alchemy. There has been a remarkable uniformity in the conclusions of studies done on all forms of technical analysis... [its] methods cannot be used to make useful investment strategies.'

Burton Malkiel in *A Random Walk Down Wall Street*

'It is not knowable from what a stock did last month or last year how it will do next month or next year. Broker's pronouncements on this subject are tea-leaf reading; fakery.'

John Train in *The Money Masters*

So says the opposition, which may well be 90 per cent right. Perhaps 95 per cent. But not 100 per cent. It would have been possible (although hard work) to identify five straight charting success stories to cover in this chapter. More representatively, a streak of failure runs through it too.

JESSE LIVERMORE

'By reason of conditions known to the whole world the stock I was most bullish on in those critical days of early 1915 was Bethlehem Steel. I was morally certain it was going way up, but in order to make sure that I would win on my very first play, as I must, I decided to wait until it crossed par.

I think I have told you that whenever a stock crosses 100 or 200 or 300 for the first time, it nearly always keeps going up for 30 to 50 points – and after 300 faster than after 100 or 200. One of my first big coups was in Anaconda, which I bought when it crossed 200 and sold a day later at 260. My practice of buying a stock just after it crossed par dated back to my early bucket shop days. It is an old trading principle.

You can imagine how keen I was to get back to trading on my old scale. I was so eager to begin that I could not think of anything else; but I held myself in leash. I saw Bethlehem Steel climb, every day, higher and higher, as I was sure it would, and yet there I was checking my impulse to run over to Williamson & Brown's office and buy 500 shares. I knew I simply had to make my initial operation as nearly a cinch as was humanly possible.

Every point that stock went up meant 500 dollars I had not made. The first ten points advance meant that I would have been able to pyramid, and instead of 500 shares I might now be carrying 1,000 shares that would be earning me 1,000 dollars a point. But I sat tight and instead of listening to my loud-mouthed hopes or to my clamorous beliefs I heeded only the level voice of my experience and the counsel of common sense. Once I got a decent stake together I could afford to take chances But without a stake, taking chances, even slight chances, was a luxury utterly beyond my reach. Six weeks of patience – but, in the end, a victory for common sense over greed and hope!

I really began to waver and sweat blood when the stock got up to 90. Think of what I had not made by not buying, when I was so bullish. Well, when it got to 98 I said to myself, 'Bethlehem is going clean through 100, and when it does the roof is going to blow clean off!' The tape said the same thing more than plainly. In fact, it used a megaphone. I tell you, I saw *100* on the tape when the ticker was only printing *98*. And I knew that wasn't the voice of my hope or the sight of my desire, but the assertion of my tape-reading instinct. So I said to myself, 'I can't wait until it gets through 100. I have to get it now. It is as good as gone through par.'

I rushed to Williamson & Brown's office and put in an order to buy 500 shares of Bethlehem Steel. The market was then 98. I got 500 shares at 98 to 99. After that she shot right up, and closed that night, I think, at 114 or 115. I bought 500 shares more.

The next day Bethlehem Steel was 145 and I had my stake. But I earned it. Those six weeks of waiting for the right moment were the most strenuous and wearing six weeks I ever put in. But it paid me...'

This is surely one of the most compelling passages in all the literature about investing. It comes from *Reminiscences of a Stock Operator* by Edwin Lefèvre. Every serious chartist has read this book. In fact the 'I' was not Lefèvre but Jesse Livermore.

Livermore was not a chartist as such. He knows the recent price histories of what he invests in without resorting to a chart, and he does not generally pay a lot of attention to previous support and resistance levels. All he is interested in is the trend of the moment: whether it is up or down, and as an occasional background matter, why the trend should be what it is. This too, he knows without painstaking study. This is not to say his knowledge was slight: quite the contrary, he was always well-informed, but he appears to have soaked up this knowledge about the fundamentals almost without trying. His day was dominated by thinking about where the current trend was, not by research into which factors might take it elsewhere next week.

On charts, he says,

'I should say that a chart helps those who can read it or rather who can assimilate what they read. The average chart reader, however, is apt to become obsessed with the notion that the dips and peaks and primary and secondary movements are all there is to stock speculation. If he pushes his confidence to its logical limit he is bound to go broke.'

There is a quadruple measure of irony in this. Even though Livermore clearly had an amazing handle on the extra that needed to be known above and beyond the chart, it didn't save him from that very fate.

During his time as a speculator on Wall Street from the turn of the century into the 1930s. Livermore made and lost four substantial fortunes. In fact, the reason Bethlehem Steel purchase has to be right first time is that in the previous chapter, Livermore is put into bankruptcy owing a million dollars. Livermore himself took up the pen, publishing *How to Trade in Stocks* in 1940. He needed to. He was broke again. Later that year, he committed suicide.

Despite this sad end and the message it holds for all chartists – that what comes, can readily go – Livermore is considered one of the wisest people ever to turn charting – or something close to it – into a career.

VICTOR SPERANDEO

You have probably never heard of him, but Victor Sperandeo earned an annual average return which was double that achieved by George Soros' Quantum Fund in the 18 years to 1990, which was the first year he lost money. In *Trader Vic - Methods of a Wall Street Master,* Sperandeo, quantifies his profits as $10 million up to 1987. The disparity in their fame (and fortunes) is explained by the fact that Soros has been incredibly successful in recruiting other investors into his fund, and earning a fee for managing their money. Sperandeo's capital was around $2 million; Soros' around $2bn.

Another disparity between the two lies in their performances during the 1987 crash. Soros, (who dismisses charting) is reckoned to have made a loss of 25 per cent in October 1987, principally by buying before the plunge was complete. Sperandeo, who one month earlier had been quoted in the leading US financial weekly *Barron's* as fearing a crash, sold the market short after it opened 200 points down on 19 October. He made $250,000 on the day.

Sperandeo is not a pure chartist. He says his style integrates 'knowledge of the odds' – he claims to be an excellent card player – 'the markets and their instruments, technical analysis, statistical probability, economics, politics and human psychology.' His book, and its successor (*Trader Vic II – Principles of Professional Speculation*) indeed demonstrates considerable learning in all these areas.

Nonetheless, technical analysis is a cornerstone of Sperandeo's style. And the type of transactions he carried out, which often required minute-by-minute analysis of prices to keep abreast of intra-day trends, were just what an idealised chartist would do, even if there was a different kind of thinking behind them than in pure technical analysis.

Sperandeo's technical analysis is founded firmly on Dow's theory. Not the bastardised version which he says the theory became after it fell into incompetent hands following the 1930s, but the pure strain set down by its original exponents (of whom Dow was only one). Sperandeo devotes a complete chapter of his first book to explaining Dow Theory with extensive quotations from Robert Rhea, author of *The Dow Theory*, published in 1932. The rest of the technical component of Sperandeo's style comprises momentum oscillators, moving averages ('I *never* buy a stock when prices are below the moving average'), and relative strength – not the Welles Wilder version – which he uses as secondary indicators.

MONROE TROUT

There is a species of American money manager known as the commodity trading advisor. Often, these are people who have graduated from operating small time on the trading floors of commodities and futures exchanges by being successful enough to win outside money to manage. Mr Trout may well be the leader of this pack. In the first five years after starting his own management company in 1986, he achieved an average annual return of 67 per cent. Since then, his performance appears to have slackened considerably. As his funds are private, reliable information is hard to come by, but the indications are that the figure has slipped below 20 per cent. Still, that would keep most people happy.

Monroe is one of the interviewees in Jack Schwager's book, *The New Market Wizards*, upon which most of this account is based. As with everybody else in this chapter, there's a lot more to Trout's success than technical analysis. However, in the Schwager interview, he reveals several pure charting tactics. First, in an echo of the Livermore story above, he argues for the appeal of round numbers, which he calls the 'magnet effect'. He likes to buy stock indexes when the Dow is at 2,950 because he anticipates it will move on to 3,000 (this was in the early 1990s).

Like Sperandeo, Monroe considers moving averages a useful tool. As to Fibonacci, Gann's fanlines, Welles Wilder's RSI and stochastic, he says, 'I haven't found anything there.'

Trout decries the typical amateur trader whose research is what their broker tells them or what they read in the weekend press and who 'think you can make 100 per cent a year ... That's ridiculous.'

Schwager's introduction to the book gives a tangential message. Despite dominating the market in tomes on technical analysis (see **Further Reading** on page 237) and holding a senior job with a prominent New York securities firm, Schwager is basically a writer not a doer, or at any rate was at the time he wrote the two *Wizard* books. He describes how, encouraged in part by interviewing the Wizards, he resumes the trading activity that he had earlier given up because of his lack of success. Several months later, as his profits neared break-even, the resumption is terminated. (However, by 1996, Schwager's own commodity trading advisory firm, Wizard, was managing $75m. Jack's obviously a trier, too.)

8

STANLEY KROLL

Like his hero Jesse Livermore, Stanley Kroll was unable to sustain his success.

Kroll started in the investment business as a commodity broker in 1960 with Merrill Lynch, carrying out trades placed by retail customers. Over 13 years he had 1,000 customers of whom 1,000 lost money.

By the early 1970s, Kroll had switched from being a broker to running money for himself and a few friends. In three years he turned his own $18,000 into over $1m, and quadrupled the money he managed for others.

Kroll recounts his investment philosophy in *The Professional Commodity Trader*. It is full of trends, corrections and likely retracements. Unlike Trout, whose typical holding time for a speculation is under a week, Kroll ran his biggest positions for months. This may be something to do with the fact that his successes happened 20 years ago, although in theory the same should be possible now. He recommended the broadest and most liquid markets because they demonstrate the most identifiable trends. Wheat was a favourite: at one point he owned the equivalent of a 25-mile-long trainload of grain, which earned him and his partners $1.3m: worthwhile at any time, and more so in 1974 dollars.

Kroll kept a postcard on his desk bearing a quotation from *Reminiscences of a Stock Operator*: 'Money is made by sitting, not trading.' His approach was always to have under review the charts for several commodities, and wait for one of them to develop an obvious trend. He had no time for point and figure charts, preferring line charts. He did not use moving averages.

After the grain coup, Kroll wound up his business and retired, even emigrating to Switzerland. Bored, he returned and failed to rediscover his earlier success.

ANTHONY BOLTON

Many readers who recognise this name will be surprised to see it here. Anthony Bolton is a fund manager at the UK arm of Fidelity Investments, an American company which is probably the world's leading provider of mutual funds and unit trusts. Fidelity's reputation is based in large measure on an army of in-house analysts, who support its fund managers by maintaining close contact with the companies in which Fidelity invests. They run a relentless programme of interviewing company managements. This style sets it apart from many of its rivals, who instead start off from an 'asset allocation' framework. Asset allocation, normally worked out by a committee, provides an overlay by which the investment fund tries to ensure it doesn't miss out on broad trends: 'We want ten per cent of the fund in

Japan. In the UK segment, we want 8 per cent in pharmaceuticals .... we should be underweight in utilities,' and so on. Fidelity's preference for the straightforward hunt for undervalued companies – whatever their sector – is known as a 'stock-picking' approach.

Many regard Anthony Bolton as the stock-picker par excellence. He runs Fidelity's £680m UK Special Situations fund. Since he took it over in 1979, the fund has achieved an average annual return, from inception to date, of 23 per cent, blemished only by a difficult two years in the early 1990s. In addition Bolton runs a large European fund which has also been successful.

Although stock-picking and fundamental analysis are two sides of the same coin, Bolton says, 'If I were on a desert island and allowed just one investment tool, it would be the chart.'

Bolton is not a technician in the sense used in this book (of one who relies wholly or principally on charting signals), but he sees the technical approach as a central component in his success. Early familiarity helped: at the small investment house where his career started, 'The fund managers were supported by three specialists: an economist, a chartist and a fundamental analyst so 1 grew up blending charts and fundamentals. I know others who have little time for charts. Perhaps they weren't part of their formative environment, but for me charts have always been an important tool.'

When considering whether to invest – or disinvest – in a share, Bolton looks to the chart to confirm a view he has arrived at from studying the fundamentals. If it doesn't, he will go back to them for another look. This is especially true when he is considering larger companies.

'It's easier to know all the fundamentals about a small company: there's less to know. Here, I might use the chart to time an entry. However with a large stock, there can be so many fundamentals affecting its performance that you can miss one that's crucial. But they're always there in the chart, because it reflects everything everybody knows about it. I'm unlikely to invest in a large stock if that means going against the trend I see in its chart.'

'The fundamentals can tell me something is good value, but I also like to know that others can see that too, or aren't taking the opposite view. A share doesn't perform unless a weight of money gets behind it. The chart tells you whether it is getting into position.'

The main trend and changes in it are what Bolton is looking for. He has little time for the 'classic patterns' covered in Chapter 3, nor does he regard any of the battery of mathematical indicators of Chapter 4 as individually significant. For him, a key weather-vane is *relative strength*, in the sense of the share's performance relative to the market (see page 87). This, and broad chart-derived impressions that turning points have arrived, and/or new trends have commenced, are what he takes out of charts. Consigned to a desert island with just technical analysis to go by, Bolton would be trying to invest on the basis of trends alone, and these would be the runes he would read to catch them.

Despite his views on the mathematical indicators, he subscribes to a proprietary charting service, QAS, which uses a number of techniques redolent of the mathematical approaches described in Chapter 4.

These are knitted into a single line to illustrate the price prospects of a share. It runs off the resulting graph for every share in Bolton's portfolios once a month. Bolton gives this a lot of attention, valuing not only the technical insight it provides, but also the fact that it puts on to the same footing shares in different sectors and different national markets and with different financial reporting policies. Trying, often vainly, to standardise for these factors is a major frustration for fundamental analysts. Just prior to our conversation, a QAS chart had been the deciding factor in his decision to sell a large holding, a decision which his in-house analyst, working from the fundamentals, had argued against. Sure enough the share in question lost ground in the succeeding months.

Bolton does not have a detailed appreciation of the individual components that are knitted together into the QAS chart. Like many much purer chartists, he is happy to use what he finds to be a good indicator without feeling the need to understand the recipe.

Using terminology which echoes core charting creed, Anthony Bolton says, 'At the end of the day, regardless of the fundamentals, the stock isn't going to turn until the last seller has sold. For me, listening to the fundamentals is vital, but they can change, or start to change, well before the people who are amidst them appreciate that they have done so. In my experience a chart, which is the bottom line of all investors' perceptions of an investment, is a good way of double-checking the fundamentals. Charts don't always give me the right conclusion but on average, I believe they put me ahead for this bit of the investment picture. They are an indispensable part of my framework.'

8

CONCLUSION

Independently documented successes of successful long-term results from technical analysis are hard to come by. In fact, the only reliable large-scale source is the writing of Jack Schwager and it is clear that several of his 'wizards' have not sustained the success they were experiencing at the time he wrote about them.

Although most successful technical analysts back up their use of technical tools with an appreciation of the fundamentals, it would be unreasonable to say that disqualifies them from the category. Like stars in any sphere, they demonstrate 110 per cent commitment to their occupation, to which each also brings a unique and indefinable flair.

Successful technical analysts operate to a set of trading rules. There are long lists and short lists. Sperandeo's has 19 rules, including 'Stick to the rules.' These lists always read as if they were an obvious recipe for success, and would be easy to follow, which they clearly are not. Different people's lists are in part contradictory. However, they all contain four common themes. Two of these about cutting losers and staying with winners are known to everybody. The third addresses risk, which typically means never allocating more than 5 per cent of available capital to a single deal. Larry Hite, a US trader who found great success in the 1980s, says he never exposes more than 1 per cent of his equity to any individual trade (but he didn't start that way!). Technical analysis is a numbers game. The fourth is 'Know yourself.'

'The idea was to take an arbitrary but reasonably broad and representative selection of share price charts and to search through them for examples of the chartist's art.'

A MODEST GRAPPLE
WITH REAL LIFE
A look at some real charts

9

- 26 charts to study
- What the professionals said
- A non-random finding

Chartists have written many books on charting. Normally these are, quite reasonably, given their authors' points of view, stuffed with charts showing live occurrences of the patterns they describe. All carefully selected. Most books also show an example or two (sometimes more - see Jack Schwager's *Technical Analysis*) of failed patterns. But inevitably the emphasis is on patterns that gave good signals.

This chapter is coming from a different direction. The idea was to take an arbitrary but reasonably broad and representative selection of share price charts and to search through them for examples of the chartist's art. How many 'good' (i.e., profitable) signals would you find in, say, 12 years of such share price charts? And how many bad ones? How often do you get a clear signal? How often a fuzzy one?

NOT A SCIENTIFIC TEST

This chapter includes share price charts for each of the UK's 26 largest companies from September 1995 to April 1996. That's as arbitrary, broad and representative as it was practical to get within these covers. It is not a scientific test of charting. In fact, it amounts to an anecdote. A thorough examination would, in my view, have to look at several hundred years worth of share price charts (i.e., ten or 15 years' worth for many dozens of companies). All the same, this is a good starting point. These are the shares that many of the readers of this book will be looking at to exercise their charting skills. You're not going to launch upon a multi-year, multi-share study; you're going to be doing it in real time. What follows is what you're going to be doing. This is meant to be an earnest, if modest, grapple with the technical analysis in real life.

A further drawback of the chapter is that the analysis has been carried out by the author. I have absolutely no doubt that many professional chartists will find many of the interpretations I have arrived at unsatisfactory. I also have no doubt that they would find each other's interpretations unsatisfactory. The point is that there are no definitive interpretations. If there were, there wouldn't be a stockmarket – the chartists would own everything.

In fact, in addition to providing my own analysis, I also looked at what a number of professional chartists had said about the shares in question during the period covered. I do not claim to have studied everything they said, so my apologies to them if, unknown to me, they changed some of their views that I have recorded here after publishing the circulars I have seen. Some of their recommendations were rivetingly accurate. Others were bad. Sometimes their stop-losses served them well. Sometimes they robbed them of a prize they appear to have foreseen, by taking out the trade (i.e., forcing a position to be sold) on what turned out to be a short-lived pullback. I do not know whether these chartists were net up or net down on their recommendations during the period.

I have tried to give technical analysis a sympathetic hearing in this chapter. In fact, I may well have been too sympathetic. Of course I had in front of me the outcome of every pattern or proto-pattern I was looking at. There is no doubt that this makes the examination of charts for past patterns a misleading exercise. The human eye prefers order to chaos. If you've spent a few months studying charts of top formations preceding price declines, you're going to examine the prices preceding a price decline for top formations. Somehow, top formations preceding price rises will tend to be less prominent. In fact, they may transmute into continuation formations.

HOW TO USE THIS CHAPTER

Each graph is shown twice: once on a right-hand page with no comment, then again over the page, with my mark-ups and comments. This is the chapter where you can try your own hand. Look at the graphs on the right-hand pages before turning over. In fact, put your hand over the right-hand half of each of these graphs and move it rightwards slowly, stopping regularly. Ask yourself, as you do this, what you think is coming next, based on what you can see in the graph to date. Can you see a double top? What happens to the volume as the neckline is severed? Would you expect the price to fall away next? Does it? Has the share made a breakout above its trend? A significant one? So would you expect it to move on upwards? Does it?

I am sure you will see some legitimate patterns that I haven't spotted. And yours may well be the 'correct' interpretation. If you think there is one.

The graphs use candlesticks to show the main price action. However, I have not limited myself to a candlestick analysis. Indeed, I haven't limited myself to any particular type of analysis. Some of the charts are discussed in terms of candlestick signals, others in terms of the conventional Western patterns; some in both. I looked at each chart carefully and recorded what seemed to me to be its most prominent features, whatever language they were written in.

RANDOMNESS IS RESTRICTED

One conclusion of this exercise was my surprise at how often there was something to say about the charts. Given that the selection of the shares covered was arbitrary, (true, they're not an arbitrary selection in that they are the largest quoted companies, but that doesn't mean they have a tendency to dance out chartists' patterns), I expected to find next to nothing to say about many of the graphs. In fact very few fell into this category. On reflection, I believe this is because, despite the fact that day-to-day share price movements may be random (that's what I mostly believe), this randomness is restricted. On each day, share prices can only do one of three things: they can go up, or down, or stay unchanged. Take several days in succession and there are still a relatively small number of thing the prices can do (go up and down like yo-yo, go up then down, down then up, go up and up, down and down... etc). Moreover, prices tend not to move by very large amounts over short spaces of time. Sometimes they do, of course (see the Vodafone graph in Figure 9.25), but on the whole tomorrow's close is likely to be within, say 5 per cent of today's close. Further, a reaction next week or next month can only take the share price to one of three places: above, below, or at the same level as last week's reaction. It will also be in one of these three positions relative to last month's reaction. And to last year's all time high. And so on.

So, although prices may move randomly, they tend to do so on a restricted basis. Now, relative to the number of things a share price can do, the chartists have got plenty of patterns at their disposal. If a share is going to recover from a low, it might hit that low once, twice or three or more times. The chartists have got all of these tabbed. If a share is going to pause in a certain price area after a rally, it can stay there for a short time or a long time. It can bounce up and down between two fairly well fixed prices, or it can wiggle into a diminishing range. Or in a widening range. For short and diminishing, read 'pennant'. For long and widening, read 'broadening formation'. For between two fairly well defined prices, read 'rectangle'. Of course, it can also do none of these things. It can 'spike'. It can carry out a 'key day reversal'. It can 'gap'. It can even do something for which the chartists haven't got a name. But a lot of the time, it will be doing something for which they have, because they've got lots of names. This isn't meant to be a fresh attack on technical analysis. It's just an explanation of why, in the following charts, I found myself having more to say than I expected.

GET A SYSTEM AND LOOK TWICE

In a number of the charts, I explore the trades that might have been carried out by a chartist working with these charts in real time. Some are profitable; others, not. I did not carry out any of these trades and I do not say they were the 'right' trades to do in the circumstances. They are simply an effort to elucidate the practicalities of charting, including a fear of giving up a profit already made, and the inevitable loss of profits made through hanging on too long. That's why few of the trades, if any, result in the theoretical maximum profit being earned. Like the patterns I have identified, I am sure some of these suggested trades have the benefit of hindsight. It's inevitable. There is no thorough-going 'system' driving either the entry or exit from any of these trades. I am not a chartist and I don't have a system. All the suggested trading actions are (or would have been) seat-of-the-pants decisions and I wasn't always wearing the same pants. Don't look for consistency in these trades. However, if you are going to trade on charts, for heaven's sake, get yourself a consistent system.

Two final observations before launching into the charts. First, I saw different things in these charts the second time I looked at them. And often, different things again, the third time. Sometimes, a pattern that looked compelling one week faded away when I came back to the charts again. This wasn't just the learning curve. Remember – there is no definitive interpretation. Or at least, there is very rarely a definitive interpretation when looking at past outcomes. What subsequently happened, halfway across your chart, rationalises what went before. And in real time, when you're forecasting what's coming next, there really is never a definitive interpretation.

Lastly, I remind you again of what I said in Chapter 3: always examine both the vertical and horizontal scales. I have seen alternative printouts of many of these charts. I have seen them with closing prices only, and over longer periods with fewer price points (say weekly prices over two years). I have seen them scrunched up into two-inch-wide charts and stretched out into screen-wide charts. It's disturbing how different the same information can look. Daily bar charts, such as the candlesticks used here, show all the price action. That can make or unmake a head and shoulders or any other formation. What looks to the eye under quick examination like an amazing trend that's all set for a top can look like nothing of the sort if you change the horizontal or vertical scale. If you're going to explore charting more deeply, I urge you to (a) use daily bar charts, and (b) always examine a chart from a second viewpoint by wrinkling one or both of the horizontal and vertical scales. Check out that what you think you see close up doesn't disappear when you give it a different perspective.

9

Key to Figures 9.1a to 9.26b   Datastream

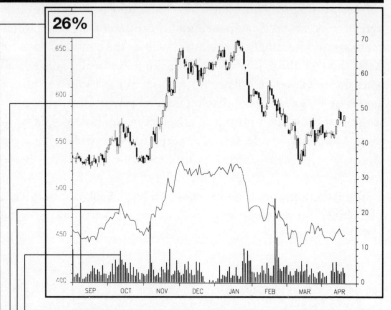

The top line shows the price history of the share, using Japanese candle-sticks. These show the opening, high, low and closing prices recorded each day and also whether the close was above the opening (white bar) or below it (black bar). Japanese candlestick charting is discussed in Chapter 5. The scale for the candlesticks is on the left axis.

The middle line shows the relative strength of the shares compared with the FT-SE 100 Index. Relative strength is discussed in Chapter 3. There is no scale for this line. If the share price is rising faster than the Index, the line rises and vice versa.

These bars show the number of shares traded during the day (or 'volume'). Occasionally, massive volumes are recorded, perhaps 50 or 80 times the average. This is not untoward: it denotes one-off 'block trades' being carried out. The volume scale is on the right.

The figure shows the extent of the price range as a percentage of the lowest price shown. This should help you to interpret the significance of price movements. This feature is only shown on the marked-up charts.

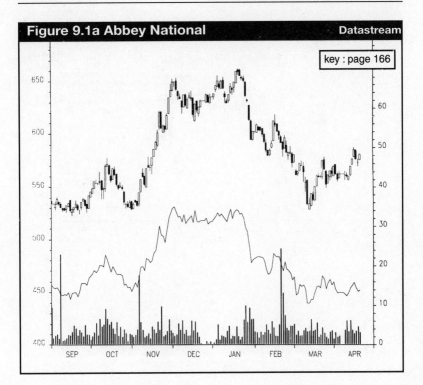

Figure 9.1a Abbey National | Datastream

key : page 166

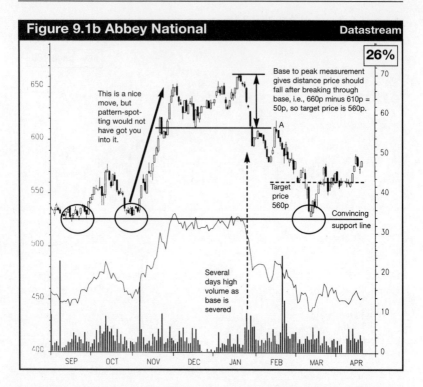

Figure 9.1b Abbey National — Datastream

A tantalising one. That's a pretty clear double top which forms between late November and late January, and the volume is quite high as the base is severed, which should add conviction that the fall which the pattern portends will indeed come through. The target price for the fall (560p) is indeed reached and nicely exceeded. However, you have to endure not one, but two pullbacks, the second of which just severs the base (point A). You would have needed iron nerves and an enlightened attitude to stop loss levels, to endure that one. A chartist would also be enthused by the fact that the bottom in March was at about 525p, i.e., exactly where it was in September and November.

However, the best move on the graph is the 23 per cent surge in November and nothing prepares you for that. Yes, there's a one-day burst in volume at its inception (not as big as the 'meaningless' one in early September), but volume is meant to be a secondary indicator and there's no primary signal (even if you look at the earlier months not shown here).

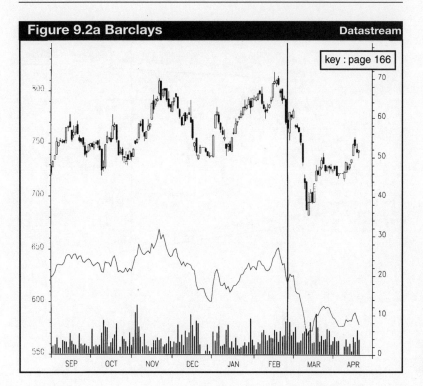

Figure 9.2a Barclays — Datastream

key : page 166

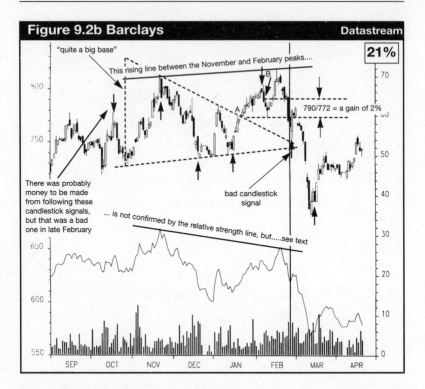

Figure 9.2b Barclays — Datastream

Classic patterns supposedly portend big price moves, but not even the most enthusiastic chartist would tell you that every big price move was portended by a classic pattern. The move to have been in on here was that severe decline in February and March. If you had found a way of being 'short' of Barclays, which probably would have meant having bought put options in the traded options market, you could have benefited handsomely from the 16 per cent (810p to 680p) move which took place in less than a month. But precisely what, in mid-February, would have told you this was on its way? Nothing that I can see. The divergence between the resistance lines drawn on the share price graph and the relative strength line — the first heads up, the second heads down — might have cautioned against expecting any further near-term outperformance by Barclays (which had come up from 300p in 1992, and from 600p 12 months earlier), but it doesn't say, 'It's about to get a severe jolt.'

Earlier on, the dotted lines show a triangle with quite a big base, suggesting an equally big move after the breakout at point A. This would have been a disappointing but not loss-making trade. The suggested 2 per cent gain is based on closing the position at B halfway through the final decline before the final peak (a seat-of-the-pants decision).

The candlesticks seem to go quite well at first here, although they don't always take you out of a trade once having put you into it, so you would have had to follow the expected trend after the signal using a stop-loss and, boy, would you have needed the stop-loss on that bad signal in late February. Although obscured by the previous day's bumper volume bar, it's a clear bullish engulfing formation, after a decline, *and before one too.*

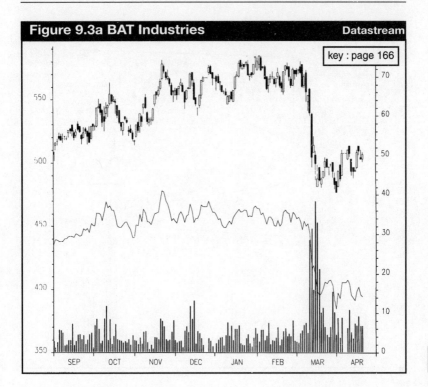

Figure 9.3a BAT Industries — Datastream

key : page 166

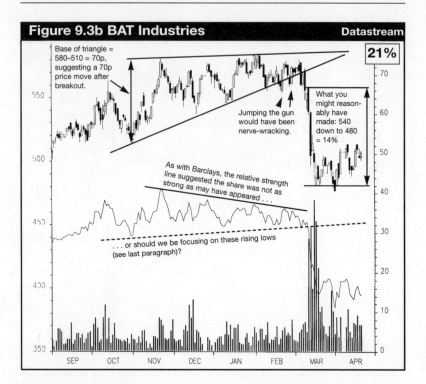

Figure 9.3b BAT Industries — Datastream

Base of triangle = 580–510 = 70p, suggesting a 70p price move after breakout.

Jumping the gun would have been nerve-wracking.

What you might reasonably have made: 540 down to 480 = 14%

21%

As with Barclays, the relative strength line suggested the share was not as strong as may have appeared . . .

. . . or should we be focusing on these rising lows (see last paragraph)?

The fundamentals happened because the chart said they would. The BAT Industries chart almost suggests this, but not quite. The big fall followed on from a major development in the long-running saga of US tobacco litigation, when one of the smaller companies broke ranks with the industry and decided to come to a settlement of sorts with its litigants. This decision heightened fears that an expensive day of reckoning for its competitors (including BAT Industries) had moved closer. In fact, all this happened just before the breakout.

The chartist's view of a triangle, such as the one sketched in here, is that you don't know whether it heralds a coming rise or a coming fall until the breakout occurs. When it does, the move will be a rise if the breakout is on the top side and vice versa. Here, charting seems to have succeeded not only in predicting the fall, but also in calibrating it: the 70p target move based on the base of the triangle was achieved with room to spare.

A major UK charting firm tipped BAT in late January as set for 700p (and suggested a stop-loss of 510p) based on an 18-month uptrend in its relative strength line (drawn against its lows rather than its highs), and a 'rectangular consolidation associated with continuing uptrends' over the previous two months.

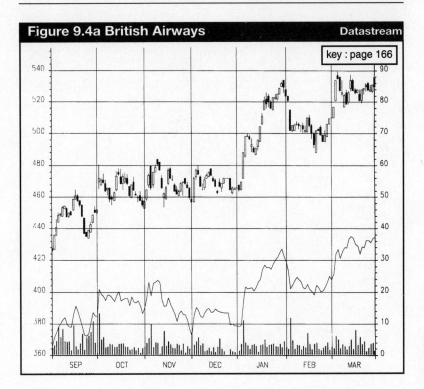

Figure 9.4a British Airways Datastream

key : page 166

9

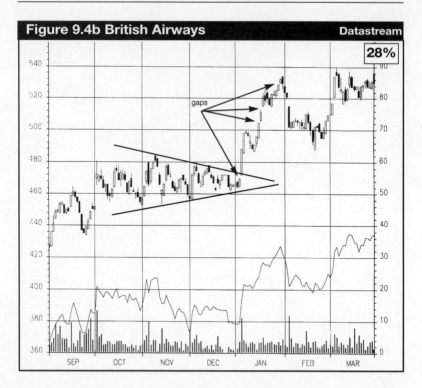

Figure 9.4b British Airways — Datastream

Here is a quite compelling symmetrical triangle (see Figure 3.22 on page 82) with, according to my count, no less than seven points of contact before the breakout in early January (and as with Abbey National, there should be added conviction given by the high volume on the breakout day). If you had got in at 480p, you might have ridden this up to say 520p (a gain of 8 per cent before expenses), before that little bout of uncertainty in mid-January would have tipped you out, depriving you of the last little run-up into the 530s.

The gaps are also encouraging. There's a breakout gap on the breakout day, followed by a couple of continuation gaps then a fourth 'exhaustion gap' as the rally terminates. It's true, there are lots of other gaps in this chart – I count at least eight in the triangle itself. Why do I only point out those particular four? Because they are good *secondary* signals, confirming the *primary* signal given by the fact that the share price has broken out of the triangle. The earlier ones aren't confirming anything – not every gap is a signal.

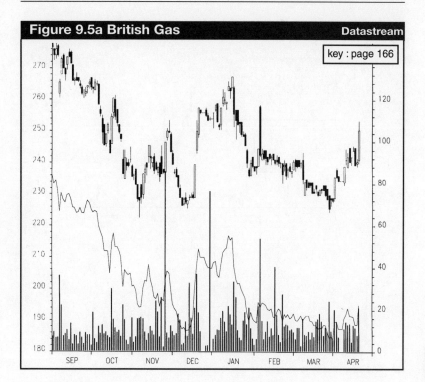

Figure 9.5a British Gas   **Datastream**

key : page 166

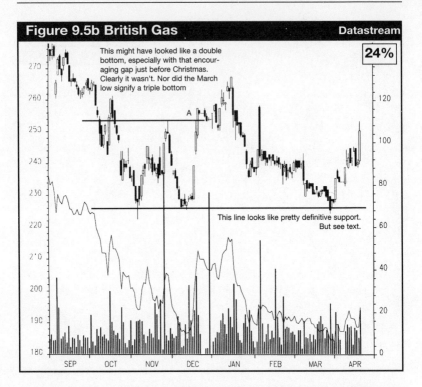

Figure 9.5b British Gas   Datastream

24%

This might have looked like a double bottom, especially with that encouraging gap just before Christmas. Clearly it wasn't. Nor did the March low signify a triple bottom

A

This line looks like pretty definitive support. But see text.

This chart covers a period when British Gas attained pariah status, thanks to a row over its directors' pay (you may recall Cedric the pig, named after Cedric Brown, the Chief Executive) and over its problems with the gas regulator and some unfortunate contracts it had entered into to buy huge quantities of gas at what turned out to be uneconomic prices.With such intense news coverage making for a volatile and unpredictable price, the wise chartist might have stayed in the sidelines until 'normal investor psychology' could have taken over again. Two points of note, in my view, and this time neither supports the chartist case. First, in late December what looks like a textbook double bottom completes on good volume, to give a 'buy' signal at point A. You can't see all the rationale for this bottom on the graph: the price had come steadily down from 315p in June and the October–December formation looked very significant against that decline. Obviously, this was an unsuccessful signal. Second, the support line at 225p looks fairly convincing when it reverses the renewed decline in late March. So it's good for the future? Sadly not. At the time of writing, British Gas stands at 191p.

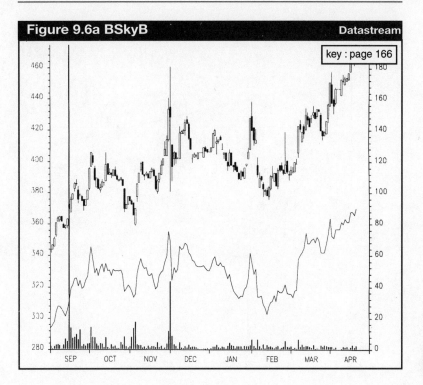

Figure 9.6a BSkyB — Datastream

key : page 166

9

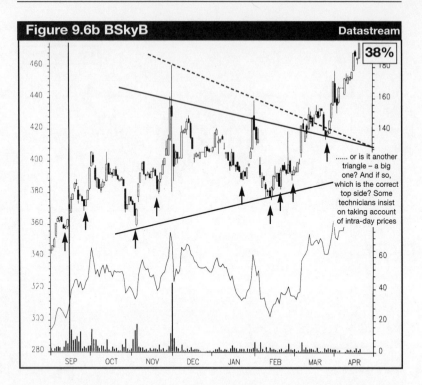

Figure 9.6b BSkyB — Datastream

...... or is it another triangle – a big one? And if so, which is the correct top side? Some technicians insist on taking account of intra-day prices

I don't know what Mr Nison's analysis would be here, but what stands out for me is the remarkable regularity and 'apparent' reliability of the candlestick 'buy' signals (see Figure 5.3). I counted no fewer than nine signals of either the 'piercing' or 'bullish engulfing' patterns, with a few taking two days to complete (an allowance Mr Nison is not unhappy with according to his books). But then it gets difficult. Following each signal, there is either a three-day or five-day price rise (and six days for one of the signals – the 'best' one – which occurs in late November, and runs up to that extraordinarily wide-ranging day). You need a rule, but what's it to be? Hold for five days every time, and you lose your profits on the trades which would have been best closed out after three days. Hold for three, and you forgo the best of the profits on the trades which need to be held for five days. Perhaps, instead of a 'hold for X days' rule, you should look for candlestick 'sell' signals instead. However, my admittedly inexpert eye just can't see them. It's very easy to fuel your initial optimism for the technique by spotting one or two significant and well-timed candlesticks (there have been several on the preceding graphs). But what I have seen does not suggest it's as easy to make money out of it.

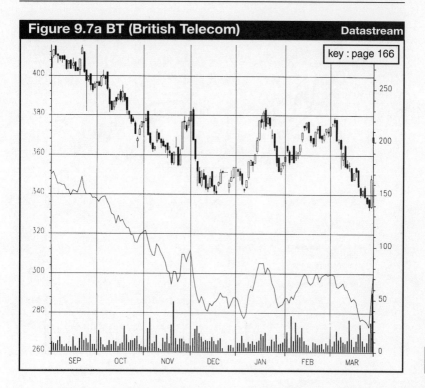

Figure 9.7a BT (British Telecom)   Datastream

key : page 166

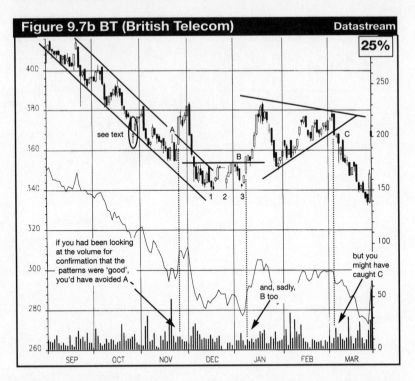

Figure 9.7b BT (British Telecom) — Datastream — 25%

A fast-moving graph with plenty to both delight and wrongfoot the chartist. It kicks off with a well-defined trend channel from which there appears to be a decisive breakout at A. But it's not to be, and anyone who took this trade would have been thankful for a stop-loss which would have been implemented within days and might even have ensured a slim profit for the fleet-footed who got out on that decisive down day on 2 December. Anyone still watching then saw a triple bottom form very quickly, with a breakout from the base at B early in the New Year. That should have been good for 20p or so (6 or 7 per cent on the share price) of profit as long as the warning signs only five or six days later were acted upon. The retracement then turned into a bottom-hugging triangle which gave another useful, 7 per cent-ish profit opportunity to short-sellers when the breakout came at C. This graph also has some interesting candlestick signals, not least that 'morning star' (see Figure 5.3) in early January, calling the whole of the useful rally which you would only have got into later if you had been looking for the triple bottom to complete. It looks endearingly useful, which is why I also draw your attention to the identical but near-useless 'morning star' in late October. It's true that the October one is followed by three up days, but they're worth less than 10p, and what about that big black 14p candle on the fourth day?

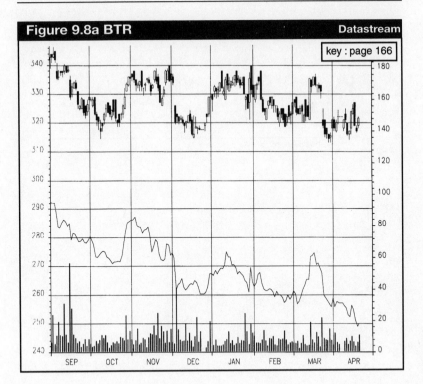

Figure 9.8a BTR — Datastream

key : page 166

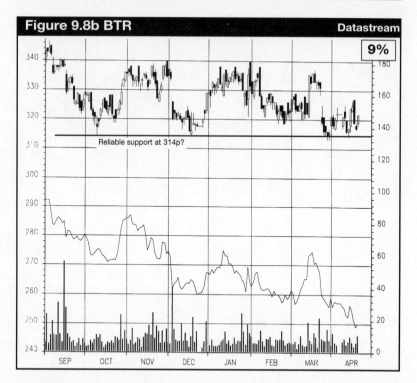

Figure 9.8b BTR — Datastream — 9%

'Reliable support at 314p' did not have a question mark after it when I first wrote it on this graph shortly after producing it, as I was gathering material for this book. So the fact that BTR's share price is 271p as I write suggests a lesson in itself. Of course, chartists do not say a support line, no matter how many times it has fulfilled its role in the past, is not going to fail in the future – only that if it does, something significant has happened and the goal posts have moved.

Although there might have been something interesting on the chart when that decline below 314p took place (which followed a disappointing trading statement from the company) I see nothing to excite the chartist here. The trend is well-defined but it is sideways, and looks too narrow for money to be made out of it. That would be my interpretation at any rate. But not all chartists would agree. On 13 December, one technically inclined broker said his stochastic analysis (see Figure 4.10) showed the shares were over-sold and set a target for the share price to recover to 338p by the end of May. Didn't he do well?

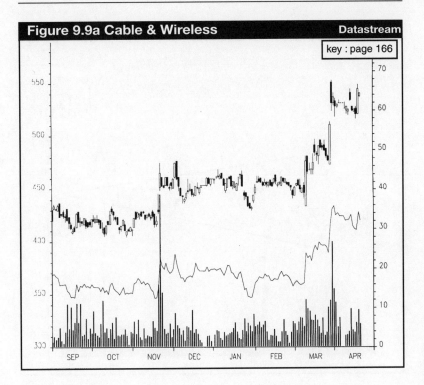

Figure 9.9a Cable & Wireless — Datastream

key : page 166

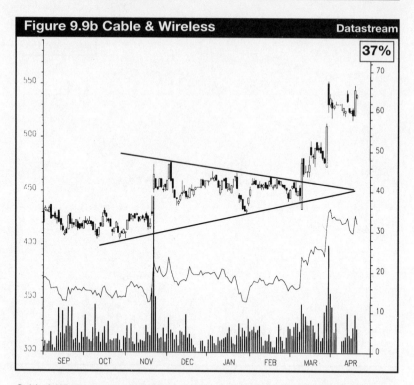

Figure 9.9b Cable & Wireless — Datastream — 37%

Cable & Wireless experienced two events of fundamental significance during this period. The quick rally in late November came as the Chairman and Chief Executive had such a blazing disagreement that their fellow directors decided to sack the pair of them. And the price went up? Yes – their lack of appreciation for one another was well-known, and analysts thought their departures might clear the way for an offer for the company. Sure enough, by mid-March, it emerged that Cable & Wireless was negotiating to join up with BT. Subsequently, this proposal fell by the wayside, and at the time of writing the share price is back in the 420s.

My inspection of this chart suggests yet another triangular formation as shown. More interesting, perhaps, is the professional view set out in a charting firm's circular issued on 22 November: '. . . we expect residual selling pressure between the current price and 485p to be eroded . . . leading to a serious challenge to the old high in the range 500/550p.'

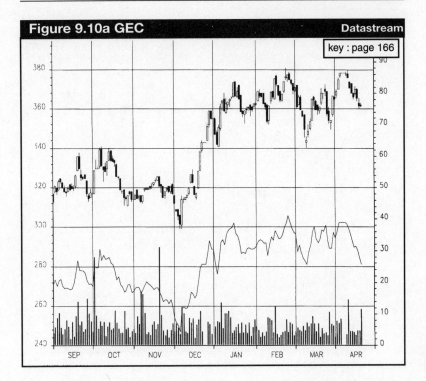

Figure 9.10a GEC   Datastream

key : page 166

9

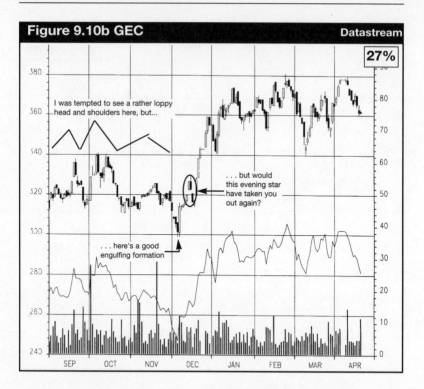

Figure 9.10b GEC — Datastream — 27%

I was tempted to see a rather loppy head and shoulders here, but...

. . . but would this evening star have taken you out again?

. . . here's a good engulfing formation

That was a handsome gain of 20 per cent between December and January . . . the reverse of what is supposed to happen after a head and shoulders. I therefore looked out the earlier prices, because a head and shoulders is also supposed to top off a rally. Did this one? I decided it didn't. Although up from 275p at the start of the year, the shares had spent all of April to August above 300p, and my head and shoulders didn't look significant in that context. So looked at in any other way, does the chart get you in in time for the rally?

Of the three charting professionals whose contemporaneous circulars I looked at when compiling this chapter, two were very bullish about the stock in early November (one having reversed his position from bearish in late October) and the other neutral. The most enthusiastic was Robin Griffiths at James Capel who gave GEC a 'buy' recommendation on 31 October, correctly anticipating an advance past 365p. He cited its improving relative performance (which I cannot see at all) and its momentum (see Figure 4.4), which he measures relative to the FT-SE 100 Index. Less effectively, Griffiths renewed his 'buy' call in mid-January and, undeterred, in late April. By mid-June, the share price remained stuck in the mid-360s.

There are some good and not so good candlestick signals on this chart.

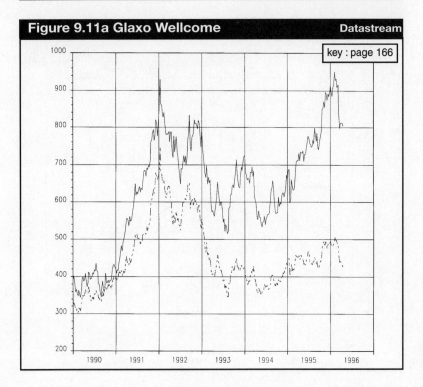

Figure 9.11a Glaxo Wellcome — Datastream — key : page 166

9

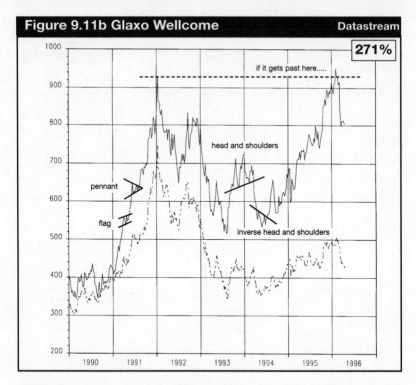

Figure 9.11b Glaxo Wellcome — Datastream

For Glaxo Wellcome, I have changed to a long-term chart partly because it is an interesting switchback ride, and also because it shows a few patterns not brought out elsewhere. The share's amazing 1991 performance, when it increased in value by 128 per cent, included both a pennant and a flag and terminated in a glorious V accompanied by a spike. Remember that a V (Figure 3.12) is the one pattern for which trading in anticipation of its completion is not discouraged. Think, then, how those three falterings in 1991, that turned into a flag and a pennant and the last pause before the end of year blowoff, might have looked at the time. Another wrongfooting V emerged in the autumn of 1992. Its completion was marked by another climb back up to the same level, and I see no pattern anticipating that painful decline in 1993 from 780p to 520p. However, the next two moves were called by head and shoulders formations (the latter, inverse).

By late 1995, anticipation that the 1991 all-time high would be overcome led some chartists to anticipate a a further substantial rise. The first happened, but not the second, and by April, Glaxo had come off the 'buy' lists.

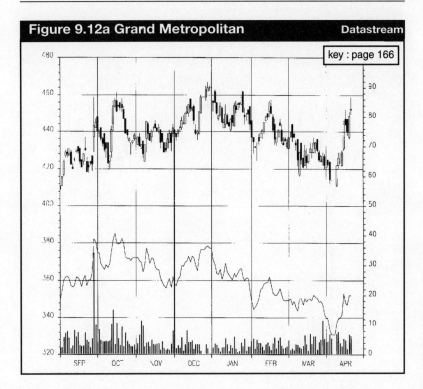

Figure 9.12a Grand Metropolitan — Datastream

key : page 166

9

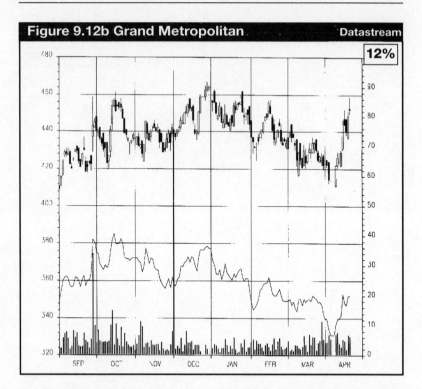

Figure 9.12b Grand Metropolitan · Datastream

If you found anything of note here, you're a more determined analyst than me. This chart has already been considered in the introduction (Figure I.1). At the time of writing, my view which is based on a fundamental appraisal, is that Grand Metropolitan is a good investment, but I'm getting impatient for the rest of the world to catch up with me. There are slim pickings in it for scalpers, and some chartists suggest this consolidation will shortly see a glorious breakout past 480p.

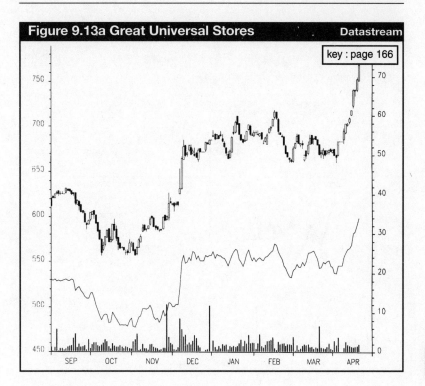

Figure 9.13a Great Universal Stores   **Datastream**

key : page 166

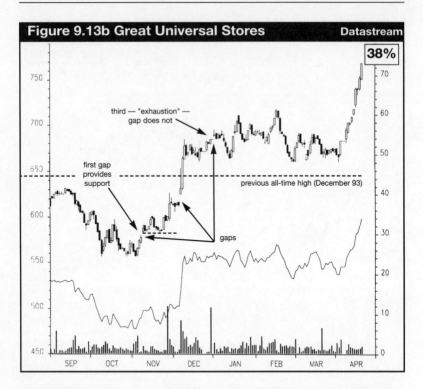

Figure 9.13b Great Universal Stores — Datastream

My first thought was that the December-to-April pattern was a failed saucer top (Figure 3.10), which is supposed to precede a decline. On closer inspection, however, the neckline isn't severed on the right-hand side, so it is not a failed signal.

To see greater meaning in the pattern, chartists would direct you back to December 1993, for the GUS previous all-time high of 640p. However, whereas a share which breaks through such a level is supposed to move rapidly ahead (see Prudential, Figure 9.19), here GUS took breath first. But, the eventual rally wasn't to last. The final candlestick in this chart was a high and within two months, GUS was back into the 670s. It was therefore a bad buy at 770p for one of my three professional chartists.

The gaps contained in the rally which commenced in November are interesting insofar as they fit the charting advice, 'look out after the third gap,' and the first of them also provides support ten days later.

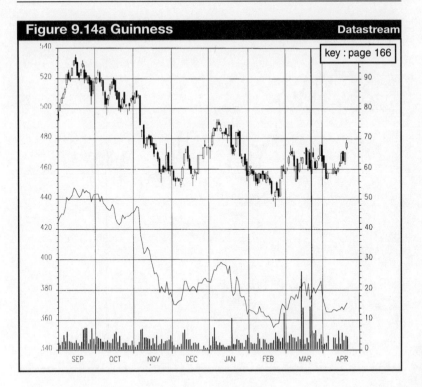

Figure 9.14a Guinness Datastream

key : page 166

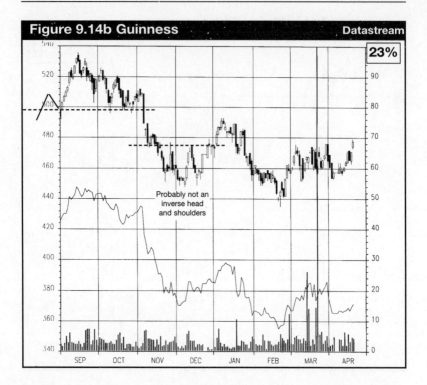

Figure 9.14b Guinness — Datastream — 23%

It's unwise to make judgements about the left-hand side of a chart – you don't know what's gone before and therefore can't put it in context. Initially tempted to sketch yet another triangle around the September-October formation, I checked out the earlier prices and discovered the left shoulder (drawn-in) of a head and shoulders formation in the last half of August, topping off a rise from 410p in the early months of the year. However, the conclusion is the same in both cases: Guinness was a 'sell' on that long black candle in early November, which was also the first of the two high volume days. Without too much ado, this would have been good for an 8 per cent price move (490p to 450p). Is the next formation, in November and December, an inverse head and shoulders? It looks too untidy to me to be worth it and the base line looks too high relative to that of the preceding head and shoulders (the August to early November one) to be worth following up. However, Guinness was a 'buy' at 459p to at least one professional chartist on 29 November, although it failed to reach his target of 495p.

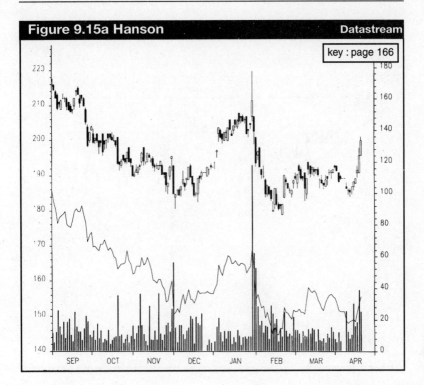

Figure 9.15a Hanson   Datastream

key : page 166

9

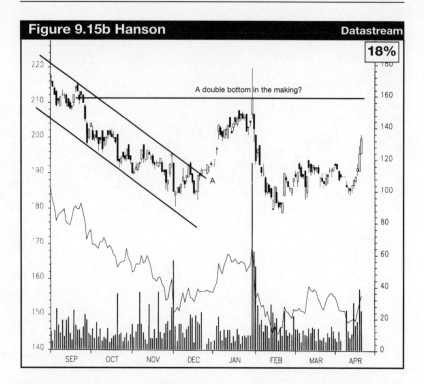

Figure 9.15b Hanson — Datastream — 18%

A double bottom in the making?

Hanson kicks off with as clear a trend as seen so far in this chapter, one that commenced in fact in April. Some anticipation therefore attached to the initially pedestrian but nevertheless clear breakout in December, which linked up on the fundamental front with news that the group was to be demerged into four components. Anyone tracking that trend would have done well by backing the judgement that the breakout signalled a 'buy'(A). Even a composed investor had plenty of time to get in, around Christmas, at 193p. He would then have been encouraged by two gaps, and had an equally lengthy window in which to conclude there wasn't going to be a third, allowing him to take a profit of 7 per cent within the month. Anyone with a more ambitious target of running the profits would have encountered disappointments in early February, but a stop-loss should have conserved at least some of the gains. With 180p having provided support twice to a decline which commenced in 1994 at 280p, it's tempting to see the whole period here as a double bottom, but with the demerger approaching, the world has moved on and we may never know.

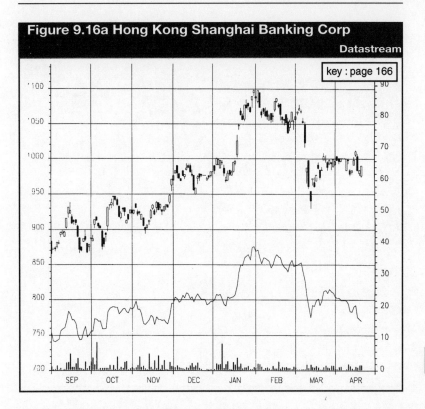

Figure 9.16a Hong Kong Shanghai Banking Corp

9

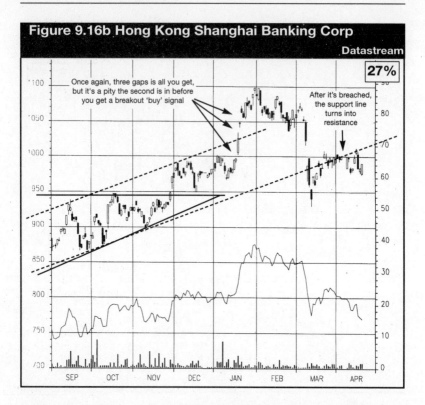

Figure 9.16b Hong Kong Shanghai Banking Corp

I was inclined to see another trend here, delineated by the dotted lines, with the original support line potentially turning into 'resistance' following the reversal of the breakout. It's not necessarily at variance with my view that on 30 November, a professional chartist called a breakout from the ascending triangle which is also shown above. With the shares then at 987p, he forecast 'further advances in the short term to the 1020p level,' along with 'every indication that the 1994 peak at 1100p will eventually be challenged.' Clearly he was right on both counts. But I am nevertheless dubious, at least about the first part of his call – the advance to 1020p – which was put forward as a free-standing justification (with the prospect of a further run to 1100p as jam on top). That's scalping indeed: 987p to 1020p is a gain of 3 per cent.

HSBC was still stuck in the 990s two months later.

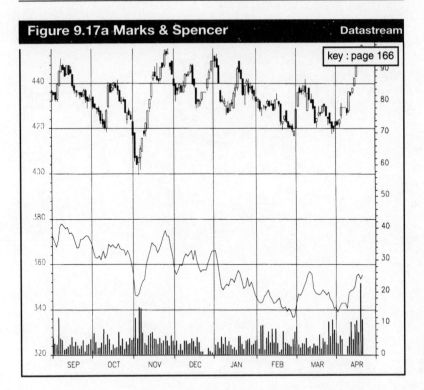

Figure 9.17a Marks & Spencer — Datastream

key : page 166

9

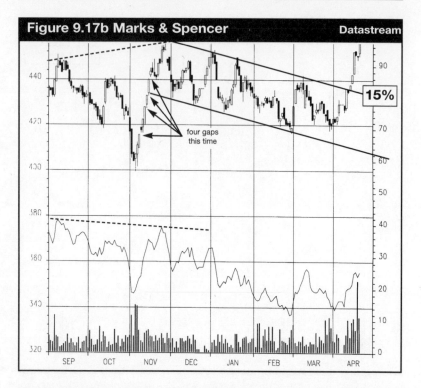

Figure 9.17b Marks & Spencer   Datastream

four gaps
this time

15%

Despite my general scepticism about charting, I would be inclined to see any sharp
10 per cent sell-off in a share of Marks & Spencer's quality, if it was not reversing a
previous run-up, as a buying opportunity. I checked this concept out in a five-year
share price chart, which suggested it was satisfactory. Thus the sell-off commenc-
ing in late October, regardless of the fact that it is of no particular pattern (and I
don't think it is a V, because I see a V as occupying, if not all-time, then at least
long-time low – or high.– territory) has for me the hallmarks of a 'buy'. Hopefully,
this judgement is not coloured by the hindsight so evident in front of me now (I did
not buy the share at the time – only by poring over many charts on a daily basis
could you hope to find this type of opportunity). One professional, not gifted with
hindsight as he was writing on 30 October, felt that if the share broke through 420p
(as it did), it would be a 'sell'.

November's 15 per cent rally was followed by well-defined trend (the downwards
slope of which was foretold by the divergence between tops of the share price and
the relative strength) through to the breakout in April, which took the shares past
470p.

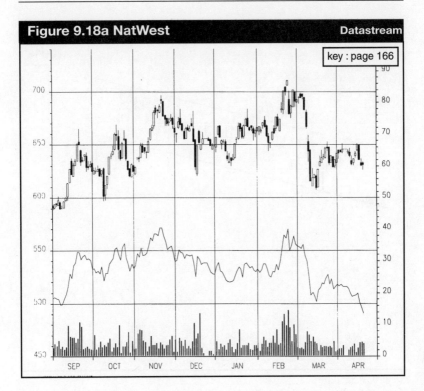

Figure 9.18a NatWest · Datastream · key : page 166

9

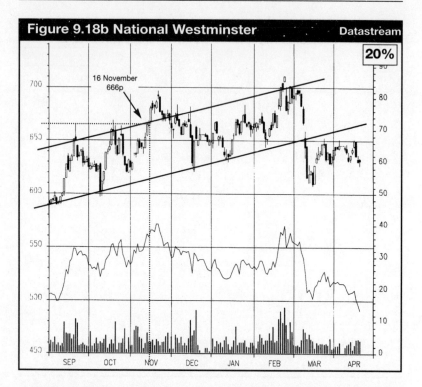

Figure 9.18b National Westminster   Datastream

Once again, this chart starts with a trend that had been well-established for several months – the shares started the year under 500p – and the trend lines shown reflect this earlier progress. The breakout in November excited two professionals to comment. The first called 16 November a triple top at 666p, and recommended buying put options to profit from a price fall, which he targeted as 625p by January.

Writing on the same day, the second took the opposite view. Having earlier been a buyer of the shares at 631p, he now cited a continuing improvement in relative strength and a favourable moving average background, for a renewed 'buy' recommendation with an upside target of 750p to be achieved by spring 1996. He recommended a stop-loss of 595p. As of early March 1996, he was sticking with this recommendation. With the shares at 626p in June 1996, he is now down on his original buy, having had, and given up, an awful lot of upside out of it.

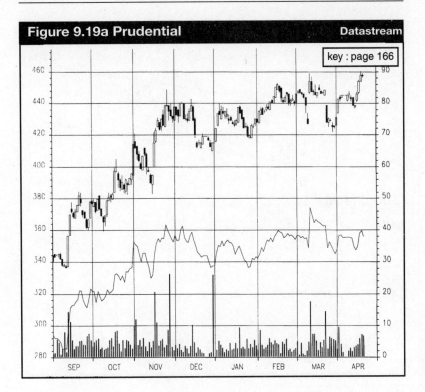

Figure 9.19a Prudential — Datastream

key : page 166

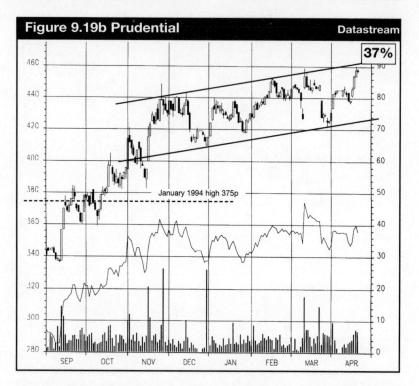

Figure 9.19b Prudential — Datastream

Prudential found 1994 and early 1995 a troubled time. Its rumbustious Chief Executive, who had served the company well, first picked a difficult-to-win quarrel with the regulatory authorities, then resigned amidst criticism about the timing of some share deals. The share price was unhappy but got going again when the Prudential began to pick up the pieces. As this chart commences, the price revisits its January 1994 high and continues strongly upwards. Obviously, this time, the 'buy on a new high' strategy would have been good immediately, delivering a 17 per cent gain within two months, assuming the pullbacks could be weathered, which they should have been as none of them are large. Thereafter, the trend relaxes significantly, and by June the share price had slipped back to 408p, suggesting the base of a top might be forming if the late December low is considered.

One of the professionals recommended Prudential as a 'buy' in late October at 395p.

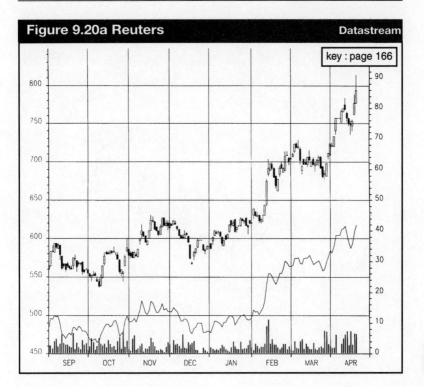

Figure 9.20a Reuters — Datastream

key : page 166

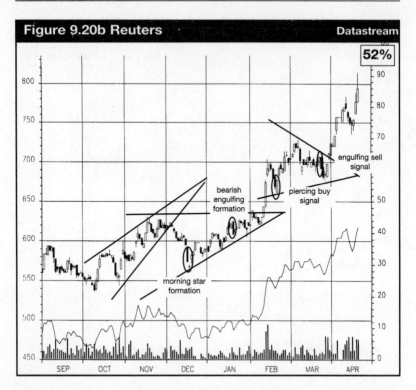

Figure 9.20b Reuters / Datastream

Mr Nison would no doubt be delighted by that definitive morning star in mid-December, but the bearish engulfing formation a month later rather spoils it as it takes you out of the greater part of a huge rally. A similar pairing of a good 'buy' and a bad 'sell' signal crop up in February and March. Still, the first signal was good for a 7 per cent gain, and the second didn't lose anything so it may be churlish to complain.

Several triangles can be detected on this chart – after poring over 20 charts, it seems to me that the triangle is the most tempting pattern to read into a chart. This judgement may be coloured by the fact that I have the outcome of each triangle in front of me as I draw it.

All in all, it appears to me that the triangles would have served you better than the candlesticks, but neither matches 'buy and hold'. However, with the share on a dazzling PE ratio, you need a lot of conviction to execute that strategy too.

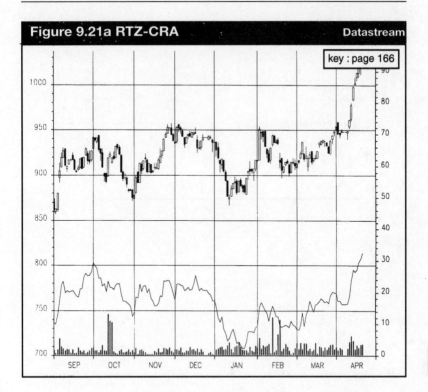

Figure 9.21a RTZ-CRA   Datastream

key : page 166

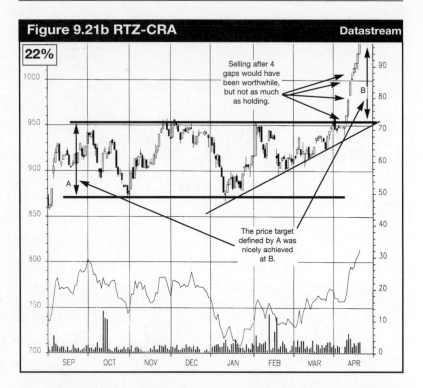

Figure 9.21b RTZ-CRA — Datastream

You could see either a rectangle or a triangle here: both have the same implication: if it breaks through the top or bottom, etc . . . In fact, a purist might suggest that, for a triangle, the 'argument' goes on for too long into the apex. If it does that, the price action is supposed to fizzle out and carry on consolidating.

RTZ attracted the attention of two of the professionals during this period. In late November, as it made what was the third new high in a row, one projected a price of 1100p. He was right, but not, unfortunately, before his stop-loss of 890p took him out in early January. In fact, the previous support at 875p was good, so it seems strange (with the benefit of hindsight) that he set a level just 15p higher.

The second chartist got bullish about RTZ right at the end of this graph. He noted that 950p had been the resistance level several times over, and that it was now due to turn into support. His advice: buy if it bounces back from 950p.

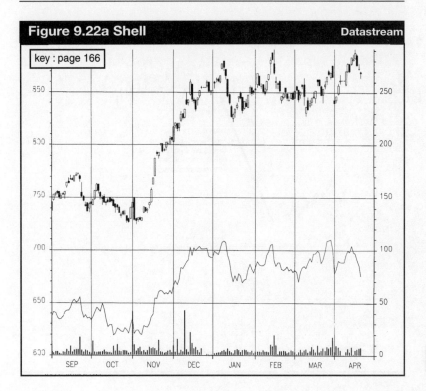

Figure 9.22a Shell — Datastream

key : page 166

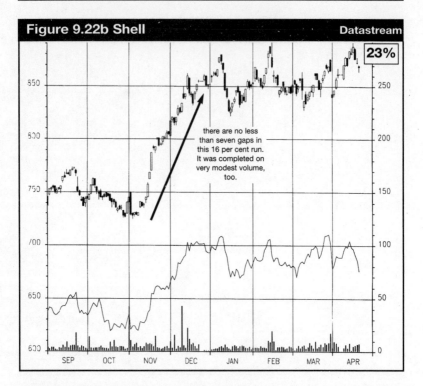

Figure 9.22b Shell — Datastream — 23%

there are no less than seven gaps in this 16 per cent run. It was completed on very modest volume, too.

If you thought that October-November low was a saucer or double bottom, think again: it's not reversing anything (even if you had the earlier months). After an amazing run in 1992–3, Shell spent most of 1994–5 in a shallow uptrend. At the commencement of this graph, the uptrend showed every sign of reversing and the low was the first for months that had been below its predecessor. It's pretty safe to say that the end-of-year surge from 750p to 870p (16 per cent) took the chartists by surprise. That said, one tagged along in early December. The all-time high was 780p and as it sailed past that, he recommended getting in at 820p.

And what do you make of the second half of the graph? Is that a triple top in the making, or a rectangle as the price consolidates before continuing up? A month later, the price was 948p, and it stayed above 900 subsequently.

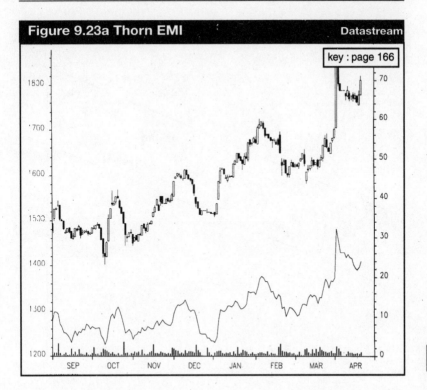

Figure 9.23a Thorn EMI   Datastream

key : page 166

9

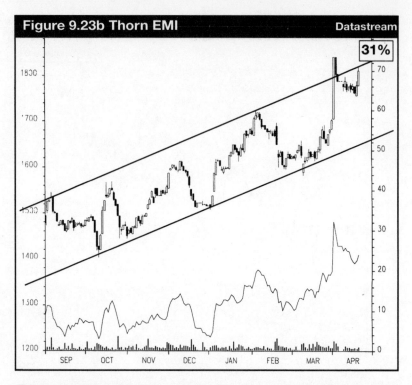

Figure 9.23b Thorn EMI — Datastream

There's a trend if ever there was one! It's on tram lines. It started at the beginning of the year, with Thorn at £10 and creating great excitement by confirming that it was hoping to demerge its recorded music division.

Trends with great regularity of advance and retracement such as this one are very sympathetic to those secondary indicators which measure where the price is relative to its own recent history, such as RSI, stochastic and MACD. One stochastic specialist suggested Thorn EMI was a 'sell' at 1593p on 13 December, proposing a target price of 1515p. That appears to have given him a return of 40 per cent on his traded options before Christmas.

Others of a less resolutely short-term outlook appear to have been uncomfortable with the fact that the rally slowed down during the period set out above. However, one liked it as the new high was made in January and stayed a buyer past the end of the chart, which saw it move to another high of 1873p.

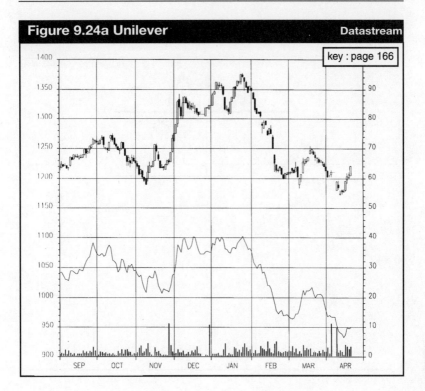

Figure 9.24a Unilever   Datastream

key : page 166

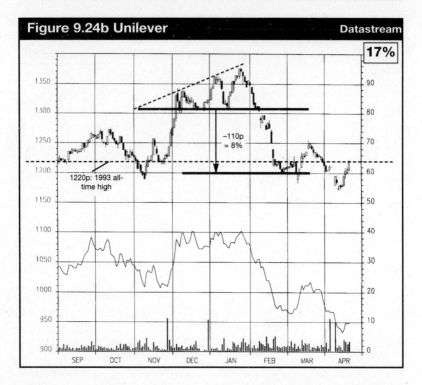

Figure 9.24b Unilever — Datastream

Although it's not included in Chapter 3, that triangle which points to the left-hand side of the graph is not unknown to charting experts who term it a 'broadening formation'. It's reckoned to be unusual. Unusual or not, if you had spotted it and figured out that the support at 1310p was significant, you might have seen Unilever as a 'sell' when that level was pierced, to be ahead by 8 per cent within the fortnight. The relative strength line said rising peaks weren't all they seemed.

The stochastic follower who called Thorn EMI so well also found Unilever a compelling 'sell' on the same day, targeting 1263p from that day's price of 1319p. This did not work out so well.

A chartist of longer-term outlook was much disappointed by November's blip below 1200p. As it had first moved past the all-time high in July, he bought it at 1289p, anticpating an impressive 1600p, and setting a stop-loss at 1205p.

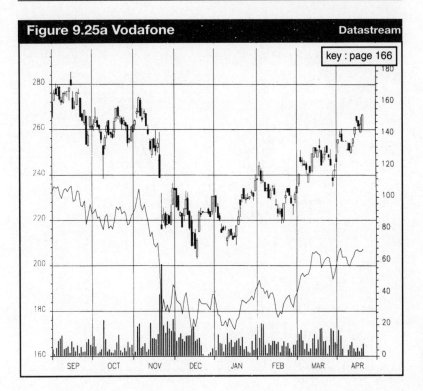

Figure 9.25a Vodafone   Datastream

key : page 166

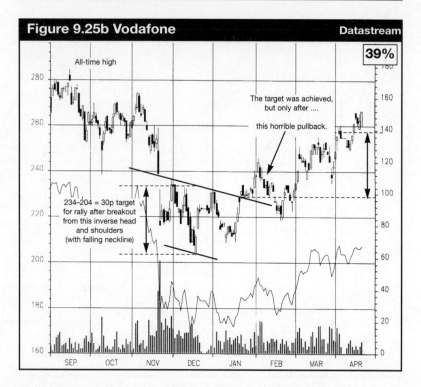

Figure 9.25b Vodafone — Datastream

The October formation which just spreads into the neighbouring months is not an inverse head and shoulders because it doesn't reverse anything. But I can't see any doubt about the repeat act two months later. It also offers a handsome prospect of gain – around 14 per cent. But would the chartist have collected it? I doubt it. That pullback in February – to and through the neckline – would have been too much to weather. The only cautions about this formation were the low volume on the break-out and the falling neckline, which is reckoned to lessen the bullish connotations.

The heavy fall in November and December was difficult for the professional chartists. The short-term chartist I have been following was a buyer on 15 and, despite the setback, again on 29 November. A week later, he was joined by a colleague who, echoing but not referring to Gann, measured the decline at that point as half the extent of the preceding rally (from 180p in August). He was a buyer at 226p. Within a week, the next leg of the retracement took out his stop-loss at 210p.

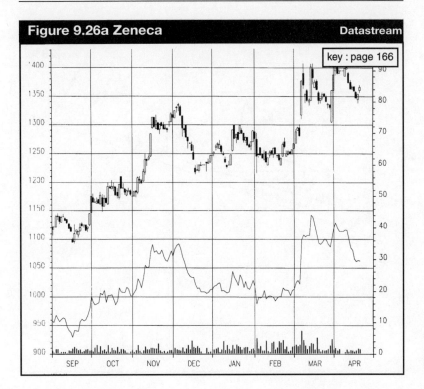

Figure 9.26a Zeneca — Datastream — key : page 166

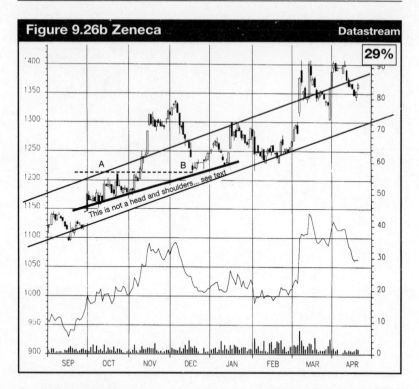

Figure 9.26b Zeneca — Datastream

The trend channel shown marks a trend that settled into place from June 1995. The breakout in November did not develop as the chartist might have hoped. At first so decisive, and then rapidly making a new high, it had no business sliding back into the channel so quickly. Twice more, the share popped out of the trend, all the while maintaining its relative strength against the market, prompting excitement that it was ready to move decisively away. On each occasion, any such hopes were confounded.

If you were tempted to see the October to January formation as a head and shoulders, note that the right shoulder (B) does not pierce the peak of the left shoulder (A). In strict terms, therefore, this is not that pattern.

Alternatively, you could sketch in a triangle around the December to February price action (this is not shown), and regard the steep take-off in early March as just what you would have expected. Ah, the delights of charting.

'Do you want to be a candlestick chartist, trying to develop a sixth sense of what intra-day price patterns mean? Or are you a point and figure investigator, shutting your mind to all but the serious share price moves?'

WILL IT WORK FOR YOU?

- No more than sceptical
- Patience or action
- What is the chartist worth?
- Get a system

TWO CHARTS

I started out this exploration of charting as a sceptic, and I am finishing it as one. I have found evidence that a few chartists have made a success of charting over, say, ten years or more, even though they have subsequently lost their touch. In my view, the second phase only takes the polish off the first: it does not render it meaningless. And although the information about them is sparse, there seem to be one or two chartists on the planet who haven't lost their touch, or didn't up to the point when they retired.

However, I am sceptical about whether many professional chartists, that is those who sell charting advice as an 'all you need' method of investment, would be in business if they were paid on a results-only basis (even assuming that their advice was used sensibly, as in, 'never risk more than a small percentage of your capital, always have a stop-loss...' and so on). Publishing a newsletter full of charting recommendations is surely a more reliable method of earning money than reading one.

But I cannot turn this scepticism into an out and out denunciation. Not only is there the fragmentary evidence of chartists who got and stayed rich, but there are also plenty of charts which just seem to contain more regularity than I could explain from my basic philosophy that share prices are driven by the fundamentals, and the fundamentals don't read the charts.

First, a modest example. Figure 10.1 is a price chart for Kunick, which operates one-armed bandits and similar machines in thousands of pubs. In the late 1980s it diversified unsuccessfully. The chart shows the share's rehabilitation as the diversifications were shut down and sold.

Assuming you've read the book through, you can surely spot the point I'm going to make. It's the support in 1994. For nine months, the share could rely on a buyer coming forward at 13p. Often after significant declines: from its February high of 18p, the share came back 28 per cent; after September, it came back

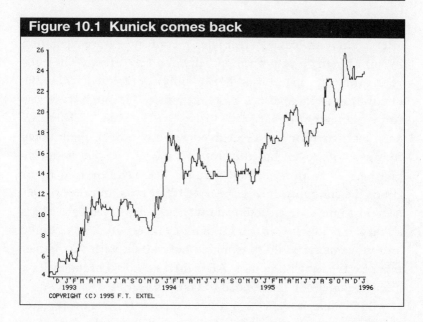

Figure 10.1 Kunick comes back

COPYRIGHT (C) 1995 F.T. EXTEL

by 19 per cent; and in November, by 13 per cent. Each time, the decline was reversed at 13p. I asked Kunick's Chief Executive whether he was aware of any shareholder who had been a back-stop supporter of the shares during this time. He wasn't.

Even so, it seems to me that this is not coincidence. Someone or some people, quite possibly on the basis of fundamental analysis, had concluded that as long as nothing untoward happened, Kunick was a bargain at 13p, and for a year kept coming back at that price. The duration of the support – nine months – impresses me in two ways. First, it was lengthy. This was not a fund manager who had decided to buy a big parcel of Kunick shares at 13p and was putting it together over the space of a few weeks (in which case you could understand why a particular price should obtain significance for a short period). This was someone with a longer-term agenda.

Secondly, the duration also seems 'about right' for a funda-mental analyst reacting to fundamental events in that it tallies with the newsflow from the company. It lasts for not far off a year, spanning two milestone annual results announcements. In

December 1993, Kunick announced it was back in the black after a period of losses A year later, it confirmed its recuperation by announcing a resumption of dividend payments. The half-year announcement (in May) only confirmed that the restoration of its fortunes was continuing. Although there was some excitement in early 1994 over the flotation of Kunick's healthcare division (which enabled gearing to be brought down to a sensible level, but did not otherwise advance Kunick's prosperity), nothing else of significance was reported by or about the company during the next 12 months. In other words, it looks to me as if a fundamentalist, having arrived at a '13p is a bargain' conclusion about Kunick after its 1993 results announcement, could reasonably have stuck with this judgement for the next 12 months. After that, he would probably have lifted his valuation, or decided to take his profits.

All the same, it seems to me that Kunick's 13p is a meaningful manifestation of technical analysis, even if it was the result of a fundamentalist at work. Could you have profited from spotting this support level? The chartist would surely claim it as living evidence. The 13p floor, you will note (see Figure 10.1), is also the bottom of a triangle and the breakout from the triangle results in precisely the gain the chartist would have projected from measuring the triangle's base. And the sceptic? He would probably not have profited directly, but it might have given him some comfort, in late December 1994 as the price lifted away from 13p for what turned out to be the last time, that even if the price didn't move up quickly, if it came down, there was a supporter somewhere in the undergrowth at 13p, as long as the fundamentals didn't deteriorate.

Kunick's 13p is interesting, but it was a relatively short-term phenomenon applying to a small share (Kunick was capitalised at £70 million in 1994). In these circumstances, it can take only one or two shareholders to have arrived at the similar opinions to produce events of charting significance. I could have found a dozen other charts for smaller companies and provided a similar rationale for them. What about a bigger share, over a longer term, where it is harder for individual shareholders' footprints to leave an impression? What about Trafalgar House (see Figure 10.2)?

Trafalgar House will need no introduction to most readers. This property-based conglomerate was one of the most colourful companies of the 1970s and 1980s, and via bid battles with Cunard and others, it laid its hands on several icons of Englishness, adding the *Daily Express* and the Ritz Hotel to its ownership of the QE2. But in the 1990s, the tide went out and never came back (it was taken over by a Norwegian company in 1996).

What I find compelling about this chart is the regularity of the decline. I can well understand that a large company can get so many things so wrong that it falls into oblivion. What I cannot fathom is why it should do so at such a regular rate over such a long period of time. It's almost as if Gann, with his theory of the 'squaring' of price and time, had it right.

On first sight of this graph, the eye tends to draw in a single

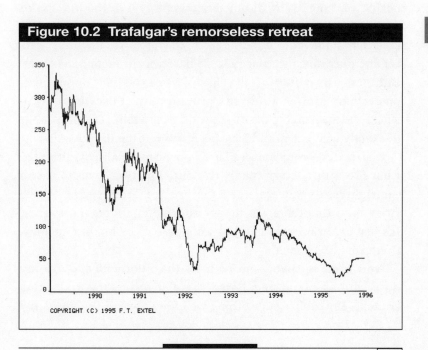

Figure 10.2 Trafalgar's remorseless retreat

10

COPYRIGHT (C) 1995 F.T. EXTEL

line sloping from 330p in late 1989 to 0p in late 1996. On second inspection, it probably needs two lines: the first through the regular price action to mid-1990 and also cutting through that of 1991. This line gets to 0p in December 1994. The second line, *with an identical slope*, can be drawn from the peak in early 1994 through the bottom axis in about May 1996.

For me, these lines have a strange significance. A majority of all the prices on the graph – and remember, it extends over six years – are significantly close to them. They're not just 'lines of best fit'; they also fit exceedingly well. The lines show that for every year from 1989 onwards, Trafalgar House lost 50p of value every year. Yes, the price twice veers off the line – in mid-1990, and again in late 1991. But on both occasions, it returns to the line. You could argue that each time, the market temporarily got the value wrong, recognised its error, and went back to where it should have been: back on the line. In early 1994, the line took a step move rightwards – and then continued to decline at 50p each year. Why was it so regular over such a long period of time? Why didn't this company – in the process of near terminal collapse – do so in a chaotic manner. Collapses are after all meant to be scenes of high chaos. Yes the price veers off the line, not once but twice. There was in fact chaos there. But there was pattern to the chaos. When the bout of speeded-up decline was over, a rush of optimism took it back but only to where the measured pace of rot took over again. The price went to exactly where it would have been without the the deviation.

It is in fact a coincidence. That's how I rationalise it, although I have to think determinedly to do it. The two deviations and the rightwards movement of the line for Trafalgar's last two years show that there was in fact no meaningful regularity to it. It's just my brain preferring to see a pattern by linking up a few fragments of a graph.

And even if there's more to it than coincidence, do my observations about regularity mean anything in a charting context? Probably not. Nothing we haven't heard already at any rate. The chartist doesn't say a trend has to last for any particular length of time. He doesn't say a decline has to go on until there's no value left. He may sometimes suggest that interrupted trends can pick up again where they left off (as this one does in early 1991), but that rightwards shift at the end robs him of any significant conclusions along those lines.

The main point is in fact, for the chartist as well as me, that the trend is your friend. And that trends can be both reliable and persistent, and therefore valuable. If you can see them, and trust in them.

WHAT WORKS FOR THE PROFESSIONALS?

If the chartists have got no clothes on, as is asserted by a large and prestigious section of the investment community (many of whom also assert that fundamental analysts have no clothes on either, and we should all invest in tracker funds), it's strange how large is another section, which pays to see those clothes. In the UK, the Society of Technical Analysts has 600 members, the majority of whom are full-time professionals. Most of these focus exclusively on the currency, commodities and derivatives markets, but their stockmarket oriented colleagues nonetheless generate plenty of output. This is received, and very often voluntarily paid for, by what must be at least a few hundred fund managers.

What do they do with it? Very few if any, it is clear, make their investment decisions based on technical analysis alone. It seems to be used in three ways:

- to confirm judgements arrived at from fundamental analysis;
- as a sieve, for identifying shares which show technical promise, which are then reviewed to see if their fundamentals are also inspiring;
- charting professionals often say that their work is used to determine the 'timing' of an investment decision: along the lines of, 'it may look good value now on the fundamentals,

10

but let's wait until we see sentiment swinging behind it in the form of promising charts..... an upturn after a double bottom,.....' etc.

Nobody has ever measured how useful charting is when used in these circumstances. In any case, it would be impossible to separate out the charting element. Quite probably, many fund managers themselves do not have a clear view on the matter although Anthony Bolton is in no doubt, without being able to quantify it. Obviously there are many who don't rate charting as an outright waste of time.

Apart from the tactic of using charts in conjunction with fundamental analysis, managers who are fundamentalists at heart tend to quote two circumstances in which they find charts useful. Both are very diluted forms of the art of technical analysis. First, if important information about a share is leaking out, the first place it will show up is in the price chart. If a share price is weak or strong without any obvious reason, the cause may be fundamental, but the symptom is purely technical. Poring over the charts for the first inklings of good or bad news is a respected technique. However this is so far downstream from what most people think of as technical analysis that it's arguably nothing to do with it.

A slightly more upstream charting tool used by many fund managers is relative strength, in the 'how's the share/sector doing against the rest of the market' guise (see page 87), rather than Welles Wilder's RSI version. It is probably most often applied to sectors rather than individual shares. Even over short periods of time, divergent sector performances are very significant in determining investment success amongst professionals. As I write, the pharmaceutical sector is up 30 per cent in the last year, food retailing, only 3 per cent. It often seems to me that it is much more difficult to carry out a fundamental analysis of an entire sector, relative to other wildly different sectors, than to compare a single company against the single amorphous mass of the whole stockmarket. Perhaps this is why fund managers, having used up their reserves of fundamental analysis energy on individual shares, might turn to relative strength as a means of catching these vitally important sector trends.

But as to open commitment to head and shoulders, pennants, stochastic, Gann and all the rest at the upstream end of charting, my admittedly less than comprehensive research suggests that only a tiny minority of fund managers subscribe wholeheartedly to it.

JUST THE GOLD-PLATED SIGNALS?

One of the great divides of the charting world is between those who look for occasional very high-quality signals, and those who like to trade all day, every day. If you are interested in trying out technical analysis as a method of investment, you have to decide which side you're on. This is more likely to be determined by your psychological make-up than by any scientific analysis you carry out. Are you Mr Action or the much rarer Ms Patience? Here is the case for Ms Patience.

In Chapter 1, I suggested that the roulette wheel comparison supported the charting case. A run of 16 or 32 blacks would certainly get many fundamentalists looking out for red. However, the chartist's chips, it seems to me, are often heading for red after only four blacks. I am not aware of any research on the subject, but I suspect that a triple bottom would be a more reliable indicator of a forthcoming rise than a double bottom. After all, the triple bottom category includes all the failed double bottoms. As Jesse Livermore said, 'Money is made by sitting, not trading.' He meant sitting through 16 blacks, and although I'm not aware of him addressing the subject of bottoms as such, I'm sure he would have seen the triple bottom as the superior signal. The trouble is, of course, that triple bottoms are rarer. Waiting for triple bottoms doesn't suit Mr Action.

Nor is he encouraged to do so. Most chartists have to sing for their supper. And they eat on a daily basis. No professional

10

chartist, except one running his own fund, could afford to restrict his advice to the rarest, and presumably best signals: the gold-plated signals. This is true even if the chartist is not earning commissions: the fee-paying client (who pays a fixed amount irrespective of the amount of business he does) will want to hear from his chartist more than a few times a year.

An acquaintance of mine who is an economist says the reason economists so often give us the wrong answers is that their clients ask the wrong questions. In his view, the economics profession is not capable of answering the questions the rest of us continually put to it. So why do we put them? And why do they answer them? We ask them because they're the questions to which we want answers. They answer them, because they're the only questions they're ever asked.

Chartists are in a similar bind. (However, unlike economists, chartists have an alternative, which is to desert their clients and manage their own money, full time. I will return to this subject shortly.) Most investors abhor 'sitting'. Even Livermore: in his own book, *How to Trade in Stocks,* he relates how impatience caused him to invest in cotton 'before the time was right.' As this trade didn't earn him a quick profit, he liquidated it at a modest loss. The next week he repeats the exercise. He does this six times in all. When he's finally decided to have nothing more to do with cotton for the moment, the indicator he had been anticipating comes through and the price soars.

Other investors have the same weakness in following Livermore's advice about sitting as he did himself. And they require their advisers to demonstrate this weakness too. Realistically, how many fund managers are going to pay fees of £5,000 or £10,000, or sometimes I understand, £30,000 a year for advice from a chartist, if the sum of that advice is three or four phone calls a year when the truly gold-plated signals come through? The chartist is required to have a view on everything that moves. The client wants to know whether his ICI shares are a technical hold. Is the chartist going to reply 'I haven't a clue'?

And yet the chartists make rods for their own backs. One charting firm faxes a daily 'Share of the Day' recommendation to its clients. The flagship publication of another contains recommendations on hundreds of shares per month.

My yearning for the gold-plated charting signal is probably a leaf out of my fundamentalist book. I prefer fewer stocks in my portfolio to many. I believe that the fewer you look at, the more you can know about them. I don't see any point in having 20 excellent shares and 30 good ones. Why not just have 20 excellent ones?

But there's more to the gold-plated signals argument than my preferences. In the camp of the rare Ms Patience you will also find Jesse Livermore (at least in spirit) and Stanley Kroll.

OR DIME-A-DOZEN?

Read Jack Schwager's interviews with the market wizards, and you won't find anybody waiting patiently for gold-plated signals. In the first place, they would be dubious about the prospect of identifying them. Secondly, they argue that it's safer anyway to trade on all the signals. A trading system means putting a small and equal amount of money on every signal. The good ones will more than pay for the bad ones. That's what makes a trading system worthy of the title: the built-in ability to deal with losing trades. He who waits for gold-plated signals inevitably bets more on each one. Even gold-plated signals will not be totally reliable so a few bad trades will decimate your capital not to mention your confidence.

The wizards' trading systems aren't designed to give them huge profits on trade. They aim to win regular small profits and irregular large ones, sufficient to more than pay for regular small losses. They are happy to run a system that gives them only a slight advantage, but extracting it means following the system in a very mechanical way. They trade all the signals, running the winners and cutting the losers. It is not necessary for a majority of the signals to be winners. A system which gives an 8 per cent winner for every four 2 per cent losers will break even – as long as the losers are kept rigidly within these bounds. From this base, all that's needed is for the occasional 8 per cent winner to turn into a 12 per center. That puts the system ahead. If the trading system is durable, that will to make its designer rich.

To follow such a system, three disciplines are needed.

1 Never wittingly let a loser run. A central feature of a good system is that you don't need to do this. The winners will more than pay for the losers. It doesn't matter that they might have come back and turned into winners.

'Wittingly', because some losers will inevitably exceed 2 per cent. The tool that keeps losses in check is the stop-loss order but it doesn't always work. Your stockbroker cannot execute an order at 180p if the price moves straight from 190p to 170p.

2 The discipline to discontinue trading when the system ceases to work. No system works 100 per cent of the time. Market conditions change, sometimes imperceptibly. The only sign they have changed may be that what has been a winning trading system turns into a losing one. The wizards often cite two rules intended to cope with this problem. First, monitor the volatility of prices. If volatility changes, stop trading until the level with which the system was comfortable returns. Second, determine an overall system loss (say 10 per cent of capital) at which point trading will cease (regardless of volatility) pending a review.

3 Never risk more of your capital on a trade than the system allows. *You can have a winning system and yet run out of money before you win.* If the testing of your system against old prices and signals shows that you sometimes need to run 50 trades simultaneously, then the limit you can risk on any trade is 2 per cent of your capital. Risking 3 per cent is the same fault as running losses.

Mr Action may be more restrained in his trading style than you might think.

Perhaps the difference between Kroll and Livermore on the one hand and Schwager's more up-to-date wizards on the other is that the latter have computers. Computers make it feasible to track scores of markets and to generate and act upon dozens of trading signals a day. There's no need to wait for the big chance when there are lots of little ones.

NOT NEEDING TO UNDERSTAND

Schwager's interviewees are also pretty unanimous on another point. They don't feel the need to understand why their systems work. Several of them started out as business school graduates brought up on the 'random walk' theory. They encountered technical analysis as sceptics. They tested it to prove the point. Finding that they couldn't, they opened their minds to the possibility that it was false, at least some of the time.

Most of us want to understand what we're doing and why we're doing it the way we do. But many modern exponents of technical analysis don't feel the need to explain why it should work. Not for them, explanations of such and such a price sticking in investors' minds for months, and those investors' desire to buy back in at price they previously thought was high enough. The successful chartist's rationalisation is that his system makes money. He doesn't know why, but it does. This ability to put aside the need to understand is probably part and parcel of the ability not to argue with the market when a trade turns out to be a loser.

BUT NEEDING TO CHANGE

The same people also emphasise the need both to develop their systems and to recognise that they don't always work. Several of Schwager's interviewees say that they spend only half an hour a day executing the trades signalled by their systems. The main working day is spent developing their systems, for instance by trying to identify common features of their losing trades and working out how if at all these can be screened out. Moreover, they work on new systems to run alongside existing ones, and to take over from them if the existing ones start to fail.

SHOULD PROFESSIONAL CHARTISTS BE RICH?

They should. And not from income received in commissions and fees, but from profits earned by investing in their chosen markets.

The justification is that chartists, even where they admit to serving merely as 'back-up' to the fundamentalist process, claim to add an edge. This edge should be demonstrable in the most obvious place: their own pockets. A ten-year run of success as a chartist investor should put five or six noughts on a bank balance. And the test should be a ten-year test, because stockmarket history is littered with chartists who got it right for shorter periods, then flunked.

Either the rich practising chartists are very publicity-shy, or there aren't any, apart from a very few who are obviously doing more than charting or doing it with unique skill, as Sperandeo did in the 1970s and 1980s and Monroe Trout appears to be doing currently. The Sunday Times *Book of the Rich* contains a slack handful of millionaires who appear to have earned their entries by dint of astute stockmarket investing. None of these are acclaimed as charting heroes, which suggests they got there without it.

That's not to say that chartists aren't entitled to earn their livings, and in some cases, very ample ones, from fees and commissions. In my view, anybody is entitled to make a living from anything legal for which others are prepared to pay them. But surely, the first question anyone offered advice by a chartist should ask is, 'And how rich are you?'

AND FUNDAMENTALISTS?

Fundamentalists who manage other people's money should also be richer than the rest of us. The reason they don't come in for the same observation as above is that their performance is monitored. We don't need to ask them how rich they are because we know the answer to the more useful question: 'How rich are they making their clients?' Or at least, we know the answer if it occurs to us to ask the question.

Stockmarket chartists, however, seem to live on the 'sell side' of the industry, and their long term performance is not measured as rigorously as that of the 'buy side'.

AND YOU?

I may have put you off technical analysis altogether. Alternatively, you may want to assign it a strictly supporting role to fundamental analysis. Even if you're keen, it may be a gold-plated signals approach for you. In any of these cases, I doubt whether there's any more I can offer you.

10

But if you're keen and you want to follow an active programme, here's my advice:

1 Treat technical analysis as a purely mechanical exercise.

2 Identify one or two simple signals that you are going to look for. For instance, a golden cross, a stochastic signal in a sideways trending share, a breakout after a 'five points of definition' triangle, a hanging man followed by an engulfing formation.

3 Spend as long as it takes to work through at least 500 years of share price (that is, one year for each of 500 shares) and ascertain how often your selected signal was good. If you don't have the time to do this, you won't have the time to be a chartist.

4 Work out whether it would have been best to sell the good trades after a 5, 7 or 10 per cent gain. Obviously you can either

have fewer big gains or more small ones. Going for the big ones will mean giving up some of the smaller ones. For the moment, don't consider higher gains.

5 Assume you had put £500 into every good and bad signal in your 500 one-year share price histories. Now work out your peak requirement for money, assuming you had traded all the signals.

6 Assuming you have at least one and a half times this amount of money available, it is worth working out how much you would have made or lost. If you don't have the money, don't bother. (Perhaps, if you defined your signal more tightly, you wouldn't need as much.)

7 So how much would you have made? Now work out the commissions you would have paid. Still worth it?

8 Now work out how many times your stop-loss would not have taken you out of a losing trade at the level you set and how much these events would have cost you.

9 If it still makes sense, it's time to get going.

FURTHER READING

Nine Important Books About Technical Analysis

1 *Reminiscences of a Stock Operator*, Edwin Lefèvre, John Wiley & Sons, 1923
  See Chapter 8. If you read only one (other!) book...

2 *Market Wizards*, Jack D Schwager, HarperBusiness, 1989

3 *The New Market Wizards,* Jack D Schwager, HarperBusiness, 1992
  Two hugely readable books comprising interviews with professional short-term investors, many of whom use a sizeable dose of technical analysis. The books give a good feel for the unusual personality types which succeed in this profession. Each interviewee gives his recipe for success.

4 *Schwager on Futures: Technical Analysis*, Jack D Schwager, John Wiley & Sons, 1996
  The book issued to rookie traders by all the big Wall Street firms. This is a textbook, but well set out and not beyond the average enthusiast. You should work through its 200 pages of 'What happened next?' graphs before venturing your money on technical analysis.

5 *The Investor's Guide to Technical Analysis*, Elli Gifford, Pitman Publishing, 1995
  One of the few heavyweight accounts not written by an American (Ms Gifford is a director of Investment Research of Cambridge Limited, one of the main UK charting firms).

6 *Trader Vic – Methods of a Wall Street Master*, Victor Sperandeo with T Sullivan Brown, John Wiley & Sons, 1991

7 *Trader Vic II – Principles of Professional Speculation*, Victor Sperandeo, John Wiley & Sons, 1994
  Sperandeo (see Chapter 8) has spent 20 years doing and thinking about technical analysis, which he blends with fundamental analysis. He has some very good insights, often based on his own extensive research.

8 *The Encyclopedia of Technical Market Indicators*, Robert Colby and Thomas Meyers, Irwin, 1988

9 *Technical Analysis Explained*, Martin J. Pring, McGraw-Hill, 1991 (third edition)

Recent Books on Specialist Areas of Technical Analysis

Japanese Candlestick Charting Tehniques, Steve Nison, New York Institute of Finance, 1991

Beyond Candlesticks, Steve Nison, John Wiley & Sons, 1994

Point and Figure Charting, Thomas J Dorsey, John Wiley & Sons, 1995

MESA and Trading Cycles, John F Ehlers, John Wiley & Sons, 1992

Momentum, Direction, and Divergence, William Blau, John Wiley & Sons, 1995

Technical Analysis and Options Strategies, Kenneth H Shaleen, Irwin, 1992

Neural Networks for Financial Forecasting, Edward Gately, John Wiley & Sons, 1996

The Intelligent Speculator, Ralph J Fessenden, Irwin, 1996

Tricks of the Floor Trader, Neal T Weintraub, Irwin, 1996

A Few Technical Analysis Classics

The Professional Commodity Trader, Stanley Kroll, Traders Press, 1995 (reprint)

How to Trade in Stocks, Jesse L Livermore, Traders Press, 1991 (reprint)

How to Make Profits Trading in Commodities, WD Gann, Lambert-Gann, 1976

Truth of the Stock Tape, WD Gann, Financial Guardian, 1932

The Dow Theory, Robert Rhea, Barron's 1932

Technical Analysis of Stock Market Trends, Robert D Edwards and John Magee, John Magee, 1966 (fifth edition)

New Concepts in Technical Trading Systems, J Welles Wilder, Trend Research, 1978

The Major Works of RN Elliott, Robert Rougelot Prechter and Alfred John Frost, New Classics Library, 1980

Elliott Wave Principle, Robert Rougelot Prechter, New Classics Library, 1980

The Long Wave Cycle, N Kondratieff, Richardson and Snyder, 1984

General books on investment quoted in the text and a few other classics which all investors should read

The Intelligent Investor, Benjamin Graham, Harper & Row, 1973 (fourth edition)

Possibly the best book on investing – from a fundamentalist viewpoint – ever written. Very readable. It barely dates.

Stocks for the Long Run, Jeremy J Siegel, Richard D Irwin, 1994

The Zulu Principle, Jim Slater, Orion, 1992

A Random Walk Down Wall Street, Burton G Malkiel, Norton, 1996 (sixth edition)

Professor Burton Malkiel does an academic demolition job on technical analysis, and on fundamental analysis. An up-to-date classic. Very readable – although scholarly, it is not a textbook.

The Money Masters, John Train, HarperBusiness, 1980

The New Money Masters, John Train, HarperBusiness, 1989

John 'technical analysis is fakery' Train (who is a successful investment manager) profiles 16 and a half fundamental investors, and one and a half chartists.

Investment Psychology Explained, Martin J Pring, John Wiley & Sons, 1993

Extraordinary Popular Delusions and the Madness of Crowds, Charles Mackay, and *Confusión de Confusiones*, Joseph de la Vega, John Wiley & Sons, 1996

Two pre-20th century classics on the cupidity of investors. 'Delusions' is a long book dealing with the cupidity of non-investors too, but its opening chapters are the definitive accounts of the South Sea Bubble, the Mississippi Scheme and the Tulipomania. Only these three chapters are included in this recent edition.

All of these books should be obtainable from: Harriman House Investors Bookshop, 43 Chapel Street, Petersfield, Hampshire, GU32 3DY Phone (freephone) 0800 435060
Fax 01730 233880
e-mail 100745.2031@compuserve.com

GLOSSARY

Asterisked items are discussed in the main text – see the index.

Time is an important component in the definition of many of these terms, but cannot be expressed specifically because many of the terms can be used equally in long- and short-term timeframes. For instance, a base area could form over three days between 60 and 63p, and over six months between 60 and 70p.

Accumulation   A phase in the market cycle when supposed long-term /well-informed / 'smart money' investors are buying shares ahead of an advance. This term and its opposite, 'distribution', are core elements in Dow theory.

*Advance/decline line   A measure of how many shares have moved forward, and how many, backward.

Base area   The levelling out of price, and the price at which this occurs, in advance of a reversal pattern or breakout.

Bear trap   Following a price rise, a reversal signal turns out to be false, so proving expensive for any 'bears' who sought to profit from the anticipated new downtrend.

*Beta   A measure of the volatility of a share price. A high beta share demonstrates greater price variability than a low beta share.

Blowoff   Or speculative orgy. An extended and unsustainable upwards surge in a share price or market. At the start of a blowoff, prices are already far ahead of any level which would be indicated by fundamental values. The blowoff first magnifies this discrepancy, then murders it. The imminent reversal is not obvious to those participating in it. The doubling of Wall Street share prices in the last 12 months before the 1929 crash, followed by their immediate halving, was a blowoff. You can see a smaller blowoff in the chart for Glaxo Wellcome (Figure 9.11).

Bollinger bands   A pair of lines plotted above and below a moving average to define a trend channel. The width of the channel is defined (mathematically) to accommodate changes in volatility, so as potentially to avoid false signals.

Breakout A decisive movement by price out of a level at which it has been consolidating. Sometimes 'breakout' is used exclusively for upward movements, in which case 'break' means the opposite downward movement.

Bull trap Following a price fall, a reversal signal turns out to be false, so proving expensive to any 'bulls' who had expected to profit from a new uptrend.

*Call option A contract in which the buyer pays a premium for the right, should it suit him to exercise it, to buy shares in the future at a price fixed now. This is a way of profiting from expected price rises. If shares in Antelope Plc are currently 100p but expected by the investor to rise to 200p, he might be interested in acquiring an option to buy them at 120p. If the option costs 10p per share, he will profit from any price rise above 130p. See 'put option' and 'option writer'.

*Confirmation Two simultaneous signals pointing to the same conclusion.

Congestion area A level at which a price sticks for an extended period.

*Continuation pattern A share price pattern, observable on a chart, which follows a significant up or down move and portends the resumption and continuation of that move.

*Correction A price movement against the direction of the prevailing trend, but not so extensive as to reverse it. A correction eventually gives way to a resumption of the prevailing trend, which takes the price to a new high (in an uptrend) or low (downtrend). A correction can only be seen for what it is once it has completed.

*Crossover The action of one moving average crossing over another (related) series. Normally seen to be a trading signal. See 'whipping' below and 'golden' and 'dead crosses', page 45.

Dead cross A sell signal made when a short moving average cuts down through a long moving average. Opposite of a 'golden cross', page 45.

Derivative An investment that has no intrinsic value but is derived from investments that do have such value. If you buy gold, a commodity or shares, you can wear it, eat it or live on the dividends, etc. If you buy an option or future (the two main forms of derivatives), you do not expect to gain these benefits. The value of such instruments lies in the difference between the price at which you are entitled to acquire (or sell) the underlying investment and later prices. You profit (or lose) by dealing in your 'right to acquire' (or to sell). (In fact, in the case of a futures contract and indeed some options, you can sometimes 'take delivery' of the underlying article. But usually such contracts are closed out prior to this stage by the payment of the cash profit or loss earned or incurred up to the point where delivery would otherwise have taken place.) Share indices are transmuted into investable instruments by the futures and option contracts derived from them and interest rates have their own extensive range of derivatives.

Distribution   The opposite of accumulation – see above.

*Divergence   The failure of one indicator to confirm a signal given by another.

*Dynamic resistance/support   A line connecting highs or lows on a graph, which is not horizontal, denoting that, with the passage of time, resistance or support is moving to new levels. Contrast with static resistance/support, below.

Efficient markets hypothesis   The theory that new information about a share is immediately reflected in its price. Part and parcel of the strong form of the random walk theory (see below).

*Exercise date, exercise price   The price and date (or last date) at which the holder of a call or put option may require the option writer to sell or buy the shares under option.

Failure swing   A term used in conjunction with oscillators, such as MACD and Welles Wilder's RSI. A failure swing occurs when the share price makes a new high or low, but the indicator does not. This may herald a change of trend.

Future   A contract arranged now (including the price) but to be completed on a fixed future date. Often, completion involves paying over the money earned or lost on the contract rather than actually taking possession of the item on which the contract was based. A future is one kind of derivative.

*Gap, gap day   Observable only on bar charts. A price opens higher or lower than the highest or lowest price at which it traded the day before and stays outside the previous day's range for the rest of the day (or, at least, closes outside yesterday's open-close range). Accordingly, there is a gap between the two days' bars. These events are also known as 'gapping-up' and 'gapping down'.

*Hedge   A subordinate investment made to protect a primary investment. Also, 'to hedge' and 'hedging'. 'Hedge funds' normally have nothing to do with hedging in this sense. These are investment funds which invest in a wider range of investments than 'normal', with the objective of making higher returns than normal. This makes them arguably more risky and more difficult to regulate. Accordingly they are normally structured so as to be outside the scope of conventional financial regulation (quite legally so). They cannot therefore be marketed to the public in general. Instead they seek 'sophisticated investors'.

Indicator   Any charting device which gives or is designed to give trading signals, i.e., encouragement to enter or close out a trade.

Inside day   On an inside day, the highest price recorded for a share is lower than yesterday's highest price and the lowest price is higher than yesterday's low.

*Island   When an up gap is followed shortly by a down gap, the bars formed by the prices on the day or days between forms an 'island', separated from the main price action on the graph.

*Key day reversal   The price moves a considerable distance on one day in the opposite direction to that in which it has been trending in recent days, reversing several days' worth of movement.

*Log scale   Strictly, 'semi-logarithmic'. A special kind of price scale which keeps changes in proportion. See page 49.

Meisels Indicator   A measure of the net total of up days against down days in the past ten. If the share went up on three days and down on seven days, the Meisels Indicator would be +4. Meisels readings higher than +6 suggest a share or market is over-bought and vice-versa.

*Momentum   The *rate of change* of price. See page 90.

*Moving average   A calculation which is updated (typically) on a daily basis by calculating the average price of the last so many days. A weighted moving average gives 'a louder voice' to recent prices. An exponential moving average is a weighted moving average whose calculation includes all previous prices.

*Neckline   A line of support or resistance in a reversal pattern whose penetration marks the completion of the pattern.

On-balance volume   An indicator devised by Joe Granville, a celebrated but ultimately unsuccessful chartist of the early 1980s. Volume is considered negative if the price falls on the day and positive if it rises. The cumulative '*OBV*' total should echo the pattern set by the price.

Option writer   The investor who 'takes the other side' of a call or put option. In return for a premium, he offers to buy or sell shares in future at prices which may be turn out to be disadvantageous to him but advantageous to the option buyer. However, they will not always be so, and when they are not, he profits from the premium. He usually owns, or is willing to own, the shares in question. See 'call option' and 'put option'.

*Oscillator   An indicator which is constructed in such a way as to ensure it moves up and down within a band. Oscillators normally generate signals when they reach the extremities of the band. See Chapter 4.

Outside day   The opposite of an inside day: the outside day's high is higher, and its low, lower, than those of the previous day.

Over-bought   Widely used term to denote that prices have moved significantly into new high territory. The secondary indicators (RSI, MACD, etc), normally have a specific level (e.g., over 70 or over 80) over-bought share is not necessarily one that is imminently set for a reversal. Normally certain further events must occur in the over 70 or 80 zone, (such as a failure swing) before the reversal is anticipated.

Overhead supply   The supply of shares to the market by sellers which prevents a price from breaking out through resistance during an uptrend.

Over-sold   Opposite of over-bought.

*Pullback   An 'unexpected' reversal after a breakout. A pullback may or may not be itself subject to a reversal. See Figure G.1.

*Put option   A contract in which the 'buyer' (of the option) acquires the right (if it suits him to exercise it) to sell shares at a future date at a price fixed now. The buyer pays a 'premium' for the privilege. This is a

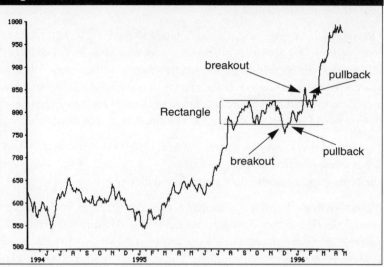

Figure G.1 Pullback

way of profiting from expected price falls. If shares in Zebra Plc are worth 100p, but you expect them to fall below 70p, you might be interested in buying an option allowing you to sell them at 90p. If your expectations are correct, you could subsequently buy the shares at 70p and sell them to your option writer at 90p. See 'call option' and 'option writer'.

Pyramid (verb)   To increase the size of a speculative position based on its success to date, in anticipation that the profitable trend will go further. If Yak Plc has 'broken out' and delivered you a profit on the hundred shares you bought, you might consider 'pyramiding' your position up to 200 shares. This will be highly profitable if your forecast that the new trend will continue is correct. But if instead the price declines, the profits you have earned to date will be lost twice as quickly as they would have been if you had not pyramided.

Random walk theory   The theory, widely supported in academia, that it is impossible to forecast movements of share prices, whether by technical or fundamental analysis, and therefore impossible to make more profit, over the long term, by these methods than by selecting a share portfolio at random (e.g., by throwing darts at a list of shares). Any extra profit apparently earned by analysis, say the random walkers, is in fact earned by luck which will come to an end and go into reverse. The theory comes in 'weak' 'semi-strong' and 'strong' forms.

*Relative strength   The strength of a share price when considered against the market as a whole.

*Resistance   A price which a share tends to stick at, or bounce back from, when it has been rising. The price may have been set (in investors' minds) by some significant pattern several months or years ago when the share was last in this region. If the price pierces the resistance it may move a considerable distance before encountering the next resistance level. Such a move would be seen as a 'breakout' past the first level of resistance.

*Reversal pattern   A share price pattern, observable on a chart, which is regarded as generally being associated with the end of one trend and the beginning of another in the opposite direction.

*Short-selling   Selling shares which the investor does not own. The transaction can either closed be out before the day due for settlement, or satisfied by means of borrowing (more accurately, 'hiring') shares from someone who does own them. The short seller anticipates making a profit from a decline in the share price before he closes out the transaction, or ultimately buys in the shares to satisfy the lender.

*Static resistance/support   Repeated turning points in share prices which occur at the same, or approximately the same, price and therefore can be shown as a horizontal line on a graph. Compare with 'dynamic resistance/support', above.

*Stop-loss   An instruction to a stockbroker to 'close out' a trade if the price moves disadvantageously to or past a predetermined level.

*Support   The equivalent of 'resistance' for a downward-trending share.

A trade   A purchase or sale of an investment, including one following another to close out the first and realise its profit or crystallise its loss.

*Traded options   Option contracts on the hundred or so largest (capitalisation) shares (and on the FT-SE 100 Index) are continually traded and can be bought and sold at advertised prices in the traded options market. By contrast, options on smaller shares are priced on request and cannot be sold in the market.

*Trending   A price which is moving up or down. Such a movement

includes temporary reversals of the main trend. The defining characteristic is that succeeding highs and lows are higher (in an uptrend) or
lower (in a downtrend). When a share price is trending, its support and
resistance levels are 'dynamic'.

Trendless The opposite of trending: a share price is moving up or
down, but the short-term movements do not deliver the price into new
territory. Support and resistance are static.

*Volume Turnover, or amount of business done. The volume yesterday was ten million shares. Tomorrow it might be only six million.

*Whipsaw, whipping A quick succession of signals which reverse each
other (buy, sell, buy, sell, etc) before a profit has been earned. In Figure
G.2 below, crossovers of the 20- and 200-day moving averages give two
excellent trading signals in June 1994 and August 1995. However, the
same system gives four bad signals in April to July 1995. The rapid and
expensive reversal of these signals is known as whipsawing or whipping.

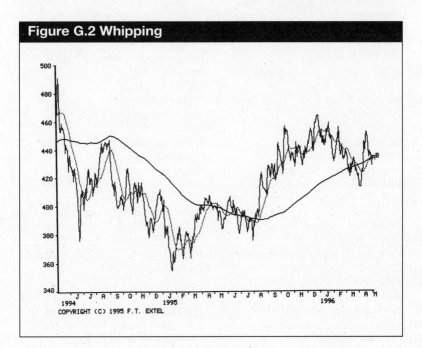

Figure G.2 Whipping

INDEX